Living with a Challenging Child

Living with a Challenging Child

Encouragement for Mothers of Children with ADD,
Hyperactivity, or Other Behavioral Problems

JAYNE RAY GARRISON

Servant Publications
Ann Arbor, Michigan

Vine Books is an imprint of Servant Publications especially designed to serve evangelical Christians.

Scripture verses are taken from *The Living Bible* © 1971. Used by permission of Tyndale House Publishers, Inc., Wheaton, IL 60189. All rights reserved.

Published by Servant Publications
P.O. Box 8617
Ann Arbor, Michigan 48107

Cover design by Paul Higdon

96 97 98 99 00 10 9 8 7 6 5 4 3 2 1

Printed in the United States of America
ISBN 0-89283-959-7

LIBRARY OF CONGRESS CATALOGING-IN-PUBLICATION DATA

Garrison, Jayne.
    Living with a challenging child : encouragement for mothers of children with ADD, hyperactivity, or other behavioral problems / Jayne Garrison.
        p.   cm.
    ISBN 0-89283-959-7
    1. Problem children—Family relationships.   2. Hyperactive children—Family relationships.   3. Parent and child—Religious aspects—Christianity.   I. Title.
RJ506.P63G37 1996
618.92—dc20   96-1001
                                                                      CIP

This book is not intended as a medical or psychological guide but as an inspirational lift. All information is based on personal experience and on the belief that God's unlimited love overcomes and conquers all. The third person pronouns (he and she) are used interchangeably for readability, and are not intended to classify any one behavior to a specific gender.

To Alexandra

CONTENTS

ONE

Are You Talking About My Child?

MY SECOND CHILD WAS BORN in the middle of the eighties. Typical of the times, we were a working family on our way up. So, with little regard for our baby's well-being, we pulled, pushed, and carried her in the fast lane of life until a bad economy and hard times forced us to a screeching halt.

We moved across the country in search of better turf. When this move didn't bring us the hoped for paradise, we moved across the country again—in the other direction. Finally, life placed us in a small rural community that felt comfortable and homelike. "I could live here for a long time," I wrote to one of my friends. My husband's business was successful, our oldest daughter had found her niche in the high school crowd, and I had made many friends and found lots to do within the community.

One family member had not adjusted so well. This was the child who had been born "on the move." The sunny child who knew no stranger and outwardly appeared to be at home wherever Mom and Dad were.

"What could be wrong?" my husband and I asked each other. At age five a child should be over the "terrible twos," and yet, if I had to describe our youngest daughter's behavior, I would have said she acted like a two-year-old. Impulsive behavior, the inability to play with other children, and brutal temper tantrums were just some of the everyday problems our family faced with this child. Most of the time we accommodated her undesirable behavior. To do otherwise was to admit we had a problem. None of us wanted to face this possibility, although her failure to improve by the time she entered first grade did cause concern.

One day I accompanied my daughter to a birthday party. What I saw that afternoon appalled me. My child picked fights with the other children until they avoided her. She screamed angry taunts at the hostess. She answered the telephone and tracked mud into the house in spite of my threats and occasional swats at her behind. I found myself in an awkward position. If I left the party, the other mothers, who didn't know me well, might think I was leaving out of anger at their children. Whether right or wrong, I felt I had no choice but to sit it out.

At the end of the party, I left the group of mothers on the porch to find my little girl sitting all by herself in a hammock in the backyard. I felt heartbroken. When I confronted my husband with the problem that evening, it was not with the usual, "You've got to help me do something with her," statement. It was a simple, "*We've* got to do something to help her."

We took our child to a medical doctor for evaluation. After interviewing my husband and me and observing our child in action, the physician diagnosed our daughter with attention deficit hyperactivity disorder (ADHD). It seemed to be a diagnosis with confusing symptoms and causes that not even the medical experts could agree on. After reading everything we could get our hands on about the subject, we discovered that available literature, at that time, did little more than debate this confusion. Was it truly a medical problem or was it perhaps behavioral? Should it be treated with medication or altered through psychotherapy? Did it belong in the hands of a physician or would it benefit more from psychological intervention? I remember feeling particularly depressed when a kind neighbor rushed to our home with a copy of her nephew's medical report on the same disorder—thirty years previously. A feeling of despair washed over me as I read this report and realized that the treatment, which did not work very well then, was the same recommended for my child now.

Our daughter did become one of the fortunate children whose academic performance improved with medication. But if the medication helped our daughter to read and write, it did not make her tantrums disappear nor turn her hostility into happiness. She still could not make friends, follow instructions, or respect authority figures such as parents and teachers.

In short, nothing much had changed at home, and in desperation I called a friend one day. "Tamra," I began, "would you call me the next time your church is having one of those healing services?"

There was a long silence.

"Jayne," she replied, "I'll be glad to let you know, but I'll tell you what our preacher would say. You have the power within yourself to bring about this healing."

I knew she was right. For those of us who believe in Jesus Christ as Lord and Savior, God's spirit is active in every area of our lives. His hand still reaches over us to perform healing and miraculous signs. Through him, we have the power to enter into harmony with our spiritual nature and enjoy the peace, love, strength, health, and even freedom it brings. I wanted such a life for my daughter and our family, so I made a renewed commitment to seek this healing on a daily basis as I went about the business of living.

I prayed. Though I knew of no situation in which a child had been instantaneously healed of ADHD, I did know of children who had seemingly outgrown disabilities similar to my daughter's. This was a physical healing I could understand

and hope for. This was the healing I envisioned—that my child would be among those children whose chemical imbalance would one day level out—whose behavior would one day be trainable—whose thinking would one day be clear and unmuddled. I saw this as a healing that began to take place the moment I asked. Not completed, but started.

Today we watch the result of this "start" in our daughter with excited anticipation. Yes, miracles do happen. Healings still occur. But they do not always take the form we imagine or hope for. Quite often the real miracle lies in our newfound ability to accept what *is* with joy and thanksgiving—to live life abundantly in the midst of difficulty. In our case, it meant being able to lead our child to a life of fullness in which she is free to enjoy the fruits of the Holy Spirit in spite of her ADHD.

I have come a long way from simply wanting my child to be like other children to knowing that she is okay as she is. Oh, sure, I would like her complete healing to take place. If it doesn't, I can live with who she is today—a beautiful child made in the perfect image of her heavenly Father. I know that as I continue to seek the best for her life, God's love upholds and fortifies me. There is no fear, no anger, and no feelings of disappointment that can ever interfere with the healing peace of God's love.

Perhaps, as you read this, you are wondering if your child might fall into the category of "challenging." Certainly, every child can be a handful at times, but the challenging child is something beyond high-spirited or strong-willed. Many times, a physician or psychologist has found him to have a particular problem, such as attention deficit disorder/attention deficit hyperactivity disorder, autism, separation anxiety disorder, oppositional/defiant disorder, or movement disorder—all of which can cause or contribute to behavioral problems and learning disabilities. Perhaps he takes medication or requires counseling. In some cases, he may have been identified by education specialists as having a learning disability requiring special needs. Whatever the specifics, one fact remains fairly constant. The challenging child is a portrait of extremes. He is not merely energetic; he can outlast every member of the family. He is not just persistent; he never gives up. He isn't simply intense; he is excitable and volatile at the slightest provocation.

It could be said that the behavior of a challenging child is much like the behavior of any child, only more so. Those of us who live with such a youngster know that we must balance the scale by copying his style. We must be more. It is not enough for us to be patient; we must harness undying patience. It is not enough for us to be loving; we must cultivate unyielding love. It is not enough for us to be courageous; we must develop unbeatable courage. Simply put: We must be more than the average mom.

If you are reading this because you or someone you love faces the task of raising such a child, I invite you to walk with me through the daily ups and downs. Of course you should first seek the help of a professional, not only to give you a medical diagnosis but to give you perspective and distance from the problem.

You will also need patience. The journey toward understanding is often three steps forward and two steps back. On the two-steps-back days, you will need to stay keenly aware of time in the eternal sense.

Most of all, you will need spiritual strength. With God, all things are possible (see Matthew 19:26b). Everything is in your favor for a healing. Jesus is your child's special advocate, and with him no child is a lost cause.

But Jesus said, "Let the little children come to me, and don't prevent them. For of such is the Kingdom of Heaven."

Matthew 19:14

Wherever you are on your family's journey to wholeness, the road you travel leads on. I know that soon you will be in a different place. Together, let us meet each day with hope and courage and the knowledge that the different place at which you arrive will be a brighter, happier spot. God bless you.

Confession

❧

I know my child needs help,
but something keeps holding
me back from seeking it.

T W O

The Day You Always Remember

SOMEWHERE IN THE STRUGGLE with your challenging child comes the day of reckoning—your child's diagnosis. Maybe he was given a professional evaluation by the school. Maybe you've arranged the appointment yourself because you want answers for your spouse and relatives. Regardless of the events leading up to this point, this day is similar for everyone with a challenging child. You've taken off from work, dressed your child in his best school clothes, and even talked your husband into joining you. Of course, just taking the "problem" outside of your home has been fairly traumatic. Now comes that one penetrating moment when the truth breaks through and you know your world will never be the same. This is the moment when your doctor says out loud that your child has a particular behavior disorder.

You don't believe it. It doesn't matter that the confusion and frustration running unchecked in this child's body has almost ruined your marriage, alienated you from the community, torn your household apart, and earned him a bad reputation at school. You still believe and hope that he will decide to act "right" one day. There is nothing wrong with him that a little consistency won't eventually correct or that a little time won't heal.

If you have been sent for testing by educational authorities, perhaps you are convinced that your child is simply disliked.

He would be all right, you reason, if he could only get a really good teacher.

Your feelings of denial at this point are perfectly normal, maybe even necessary, in the process of adjusting and accepting the child as he is. But this is not the destination of your journey: it is only a stopping place. Before you reach the end of your struggles, you may experience a myriad of unpleasant emotions and thoughts about the diagnosis of your child.

You may feel angry. At whom isn't always clear. Sometimes it's the school, sometimes it's your husband, and sometimes it's your child. You may seek ways to blame others, continually bringing to light how someone else's actions brought this malady upon your child. Often you blame your spouse for not giving the child enough attention, for not caring enough about your work load. Or maybe you blame a distant relative for passing the suspected inheritance factor to your child.

Perhaps you close yourself up in the house, not willing to face an unkind world that doesn't understand you and your child. Or maybe you begin the circuit of tracking down little known cures and therapies.

Sometimes you feel guilty. You think if only you had given birth to your child when you were younger or older, or if only you'd been really happy with the idea of motherhood, things would have been different.

Frequently, parents experience fear at the time of diagnosis. Our fears are more than substantiated by criminal statistics and unemployment reports.

Finally, we feel sad, and we mourn what could have been, envying what other people actually have.

Any one of these emotions can keep a mother from seeking professional help or make her feel rotten after having done so. It's important to realize that what we gain in knowledge by obtaining a diagnosis is usually worth a great deal more than clinging to what we suspect.

For one thing, your child's diagnosis gives you direction. Once you know what is behind your child's behavior problem, there are specific things you can do to help make things better, such as create routines at home and make special requests of his school. Plus, having a diagnosis of a disorder with specific characteristics gives you permission to relax a little. Now, even though you will still work on improving the problem, you may find that you can accept having to work on it without as much anger because now you know the reason for the problem.

Of course, some parents balk at the idea of seeking a diagnosis. They are uncomfortable with the idea of another person knowing about their family life. I encourage you to resist the urge to avoid help because of a desire for privacy. Instead, select a professional you can talk with easily and trust to remain confidential. Your candid relationship with this person will be invaluable in problem solving and will stimulate productive discussions between you and your husband so that you can deal constructively with the problem.

Occasionally we may fear that our visit to the doctor or psychologist may not produce a diagnosis because there may not be anything wrong, after all. Perhaps your child is simply the product of poor discipline.

When you have reached the point of going for a professional opinion, it's unlikely that the problem is only a lack of discipline. If it is, be comforted by the knowledge that while all of society helped create the problem, *you* can now take control to correct it. Your journey will be on an easier path than those of us whose children have a physiological disorder.

There is no question that the day of your child's diagnosis will be one you won't forget. But remember that the peace God gives us conquers fearful emotions. Through him, we can use the hesitancy now surrounding us to form a passageway of self-knowledge to help us understand our emotions and lead us on with courage. We can face this day of diagnosis as the first step toward situating our child in his future of success.

I will not be afraid, for you are close beside me, guarding, guiding all the way.

Psalm 23:4b

A Practical Idea

Perhaps you are wondering what happens when you take your child to a physician or psychologist for an evaluation of his behavior. Maybe you have already taken your child for such an evaluation but feel uncomfortable because your child's experience was different than your friend's child's. Actually, what happens will depend upon the philosophy of the professional involved.

Physicians usually base a diagnosis of a behavior disorder on the patient's history. Sometimes psychological testing may be required, but not always. Sometimes other medical tests, such as a blood test or an EEG, are ordered simply to rule out the possibility of something else causing the problem. Your medical doctor may be the one to recommend a psychologist for behavioral modification training or psychotherapy.

No matter what the procedure for diagnosis at your physician's office, it is a good idea to take a pen and notepad to this and every subsequent visit to his office. You will want to write down what he says so that you can recall it once you're home.

Overall, this diagnostic visit should be a positive, comforting occasion during which you release your fears and gain fresh hope.

Dear Father, let me not be afraid to find out the truth. Give me the courage to keep on learning. Amen.

Confession

❧

I spend hours going over and over the
details of my child's diagnosis. I guess I
believe that if only I could solve the
puzzle as to why God allowed this
to come about, I could take it into
my own hands and make it all right.

THREE

~ぷ~

Questions–Boy Do
We Have Questions!

DOES THE MOTHER OF a challenging child ever stop questioning why? Perhaps. But not for many years into the journey, and not until she learns to accept and live within God's plan.

In the beginning, our head practically explodes with the mystery of our youngster's malady. We have hundreds of questions and we want each one of them answered. We want to know whose fault it is. "Is it from his side or mine?" We want to know the cause. "Was it from sleeping under an electric blanket during my pregnancy or eating a diet of convenience food?" We want to know the prognosis. "Will my child go to college? Get married?" We want reassurance that it isn't our fault—that whatever happened would have happened regardless of any action on our part. And, of course, we want to know the purpose of our suffering because to know this would give clarity and meaning to our life.

As we move through the different stages of accepting the idea that our child has a legitimate disorder, we go from expert to expert searching for answers that will help us turn things around. And if we're lucky, we may actually uncover a few medical and behavioral therapies that seem to help. This is time well spent. Truly we want every benefit possible for our child on his journey to wholeness.

But from here, we find ourselves going further off course and onto the fringes of proven knowledge. We may toss out the microwave, shun foods with additives, and try a variety of vitamin and mineral combinations before finally coming full circle and acknowledging that we are down to the fact that no one knows why our challenging child struggles. This is a significant milestone in our journey: This is the moment we admit that one of the best ways we can help our child is to stop questioning and to start living the life we've been given.

This does not mean we must never envision a brighter future for our child. It does suggest that without accepting and facing some of the issues we are now confronting, we can hardly expect to lead our child to whatever degree of success God decides to give him.

There are some good reasons for adopting an attitude of acceptance. For one thing, when we're looking for answers, our search can become an unhealthy obsession. Suddenly we have forgotten the child and his everyday needs—the questions are more interesting, the probing more fun. Never mind the good we could accomplish with this child at home. Going from appointment to appointment and talking with experts is stimulating and invigorating to our psyche. Nor does it matter, at this point, that other family members feel neglected or that the household stands in shambles. We are oblivious to the fact that our outward search has made us preoccupied with our problem in an inward, self-centered way.

Another reason that dwelling on our unanswered questions can be harmful is that the more we think about an issue, the more we endorse its existence. As we talk about our problem or situation in the process of searching for answers, we literally put energy behind the problem. Though I didn't understand it at the time, I used to experience this phenomenon with my own daughter when interested family members visited our home. As we sat around the kitchen table discussing my child's problem, I was momentarily comforted by my family's interest. But I began to notice that after our guests were gone, my daughter's behavior was even more hyper and uncontrollable. I was actually assisting the problem by giving it viability.

Finally, when we do reach acceptance and stop questioning, we can put more energy into demonstrating the love of Christ to our challenging child, not to mention maintaining a household that nurtures the whole family.

There is an interesting story in the Bible about a woman who understood the importance of accepting God's plan. Her child's name was Samson. You probably know his story well, but his mother's lesser known role in the story is both remarkable and inspiring (see Judges 13-16). This woman, who is described only as the wife of Manoah, was visited by an angel who not only told her she would soon conceive a male child, but even told her what to eat and drink during her pregnancy. In addition, the angel told the woman that she should never cut the child's hair because he was to be dedicated to the Lord from the day of his birth. Her child would begin the liberation of Israel from the Philistines.

The woman accepted the angel's words at face value and was not afraid, but her husband was skeptical. When he asked the angel his name, the angel wouldn't tell him, presumably because the mystery surrounding the event was too great for Manoah's comprehension. Could this be the rationale behind our own unanswered questions?

At any rate, here is a story that leaves plenty of room for creative imagination. While the Bible doesn't indicate that Samson was a headstrong or overzealous child, it does say that God blessed him and that the Spirit of the Lord began to excite Samson whenever he visited the army parade grounds.

At this point in the story, I always envision a young Samson, walking excitedly beside his father. Was he perhaps too excited? Did his mother worry because he ran full-speed ahead, never listening to her soft-spoken words of caution? Did she fear for his judgment? Did she cry at his apparent willful nature? The Bible doesn't give a hint. But later, when Samson falls in love with a Philistine girl, the Bible does tell us that his parents objected. Samson was not touched by their pleas to consider a more suitable bride. We can almost hear the voice of our own challenging child in his answer: "She is the one I want. Get her for me."

Thus began Samson's cycle of violence in which he utilized his God-given strength until he met his death. His colorful life story is one of blood and gore, and it's difficult at first glance to find God's purpose in what seems to be the wild behavior of a madman. But God did have a plan for Samson, and within that plan, Samson was made just the way God wanted and needed him to be. So were his parents. While it would have been within their parental rights to change the course of Samson's life, God ordained that they wouldn't. Take, for instance, the issue of Samson's Philistine wife. His parents could have refused to give in to their child's request, but they didn't because they were already a part of God's plan. (Remember this the next time someone criticizes you for following your inner voice and giving in to your child's desires.)

Samson's story doesn't mean we can write off unacceptable behavior in the name of the Lord. (Samson would probably have had a happier ending had he not given in so readily to his personal impulses.) But the story does show us that when questions are unanswered and things don't make sense, we can choose to be like Manoah's wife and become accepting, obedient, and brave because of our belief in God's plan and our willingness to be a part of it.

We can accept God's plan because we know it to be perfect and right, no matter how difficult or unbelievable it may appear to be. We can obey the teachings of Christ so that through us our youngster is thoroughly filled with a love for and knowledge of his Savior. We can bravely buck against a world that will look askance at a mother who is perfectly happy with a child that swims against the tide.

As we wait for God to bring about his plan for our child, we don't have to worry that our little one's outcome will be as grave as Samson's. (Remember, Old Testament stories don't have the saving grace of Jesus Christ in them.) We can be certain that his plan for our child will bring honor and glory to our Lord. We can be certain that it is a good plan—no questions asked.

> The Lord will work out his plans for my life—
> for your lovingkindness Lord, continues forever.
>
> **Psalm 138:8a**

A Practical Idea

All children love to look at their baby book or the family picture album that holds their baby pictures. Whenever you and your child need to be reminded that he is indeed a part of God's plan, look through one of these books and read the following Scripture as a part of his bedtime routine. Chances are good this will put you both in a calmer, happier frame of mind as you say the last good-nights.

> You made all the delicate, inner parts of my body, and knit them together in my mother's womb. Thank you for making me so wonderfully complex! It is amazing to think about. Your workmanship is marvelous—and how well I know it. You were there while I was being formed in utter seclusion! You saw me before I was born and scheduled each day of my life before I began to breathe. Every day was recorded in your Book!
>
> **Psalm 139:13-16**

Dear Jesus, thank you for making me and my challenging child a part of your overall plan. I accept this with the determination to bring honor and glory to your kingdom. Amen.

Confession

❧

I don't know what to do with
this very different child.

FOUR

What's a Mother to Do?

What do you do with a child who...

- doesn't stop talking
- doesn't pay attention
- doesn't listen
- doesn't respect authority
- doesn't think before he speaks

A child who...

- cannot get dressed on time for school without assistance
- prefers to play with children much younger than himself
- leaves a trail of toys, books, and other belongings behind him
- throws tantrums in public places

A child who is

- usually demanding—sometimes quite charming
- always consuming—sometimes plain lovable
- sensitive and wise beyond his years, but who remains childishly immature in other areas of life.

A child who is...

- intelligent to the point of amazement, yet can't keep up with his school work
- upset by change

A child who is always a challenge.

What's a Mother to Do?

* * * *

Assuming she has already tapped into professional help, what, indeed, does the mother of a challenging child do? How does she know what action is best? How does she know which choices to make? How does she simply make it through the day?

Would it surprise you to learn that the Bible is full of good answers for a person in this position? Here are five key suggestions.

• **Learn to overlook the unimportant issues.**

Parents and teachers often have a difficult time with the idea of "overlooking" because it can easily be mistaken as a form of inconsistent disciplinary action. It's important for us to remember that consistency does not mean the adult always has his own way. Look up *consistent* in your dictionary; its definition may surprise you. The *American Heritage Dictionary of the English Language* defines the word as:

1. Agreeing; compatible, not contradictory;
2. Conforming to the same principles or course of action.

When common sense indicates that a little deviation in the plan of action might be more helpful than stubbornly keeping to the "rules," a parent goes a long way toward living happily and compatibly with her challenging child.

Yes, it would be wonderful if Jason came the first time you called him. And certainly it would be nice if Brooke would wear matching clothes instead of always looking so thrown together. But learning to let go of little things for the sake of the big picture together will make life a great deal more pleasant for everyone in the family. It also saves you from having to win every battle—a real bonus considering that direct confrontations with challenging children only become power struggles in which both parties lose.

Don't think of "overlooking" as giving in. View your action as an unspoken agreement of compatibility.

Hatred stirs old quarrels, but love overlooks insults.

Proverbs 10:12

• **Always believe the best.**

While parents are usually quick to defend their children against outside criticism, the longer a family struggles with a challenging child, the more willing it becomes to accept such complaints. We reach a point at which nothing surprises us. We have no more explanations or suggestions. Instead of feeling concerned for our child's welfare, at this point we are likely to join the authority figure's attack against him.

May I make a suggestion? How about giving your child the benefit of a doubt? That's right. Give him some slack. Would it be so terrible to believe his side of the story? It does not mean compromising your own values; it means that you judge your child as you would want to be judged.

Oh, yes, I know you've grown accustomed to the idea that your child is usually in the wrong. You'd rather face it up front than to meet embarrassment. But let's back up and start at the beginning. A good rule of thumb is: Don't take sides until you've talked to everyone involved. Even then, keep an open mind. It's possible your child really didn't start the trouble, but because he has the loudest mouth, the hardest punch, and lacks savvy, he always gets left holding the "ball." It's also possible that from where he stands developmentally, things happen differently in his eyes than in others. There is a Scripture that says all this much better than I can.

If you love someone you will be loyal to him no matter what the cost. You will always believe in him, always expect the best of him, and always stand your ground in defending him.

1 Corinthians 13:7

- **Choose to live the Christ-style, rather than a popular lifestyle.**

God does have a plan for our children's lives. But this plan must be working in us before we can get it to work in our children. What do I mean? Simply this: We must practice what we preach.

We can't be impulsive, aggressive, and loud. We can't interrupt, blame others, or disrespect authority. We can't straddle the fence when Christian values are at issue. While we may only do it once, and only when we're tired, to the child who sees his parent as the center of his universe, that one time grants him permission to do the same thing. In short, we have to choose God's plan for our life and agree to live by it.

Turn me away from wanting any other plan than yours. Revive my heart toward you. Reassure me that your promises are for me, for I trust and revere you.

Psalm 119:37-38

- **Renew yourself daily.**

The mother of a challenging child must have daily renewal in her spiritual life by taking time to meet with God. Find thirty minutes you can absolutely designate to the Lord. Early morning hours are usually a good time to use the kitchen table to spread out your Bible and prayer journal and have a cup of coffee. A quiet time before bed is another option for the woman who never has a moment to herself. A Bible study plan and the use of Scripture cards for memorization are good ways to ensure daily spiritual renewal.

• **Love, love, love.**

Nothing can overcome more obstacles than simple acts of love. Practice loving your special child as Christ loves you—with an everlasting love that builds character through kindness.

I have loved you, O my people, with an everlasting love; with loving-kindness I have drawn you to me.

Jeremiah 31:3b

A Practical Idea Rearing any child calls for an outpouring of energy and effort, but raising a challenging child requires energy and effort plus. This much you know. What you might be unsure of is how you will ever have enough energy to put into the effort. You might be happy to learn that you can actually supply the energy in question by developing personal stamina through daily training.

Think of the conflict this child creates as a type of athletic contest. Your training before the conflict will better enable you to meet the challenge. An athlete would tell you this is not something to do in an evening or even a week. It takes time to get into shape—months and months of it. Your level of fitness will depend on how long you continue your training.

In the case of handling a disruptive child, your training should consist of Bible study, prayer, and times of introspection so that the abilities you need to handle a particular crisis will come to you easily and naturally.

Break your training into manageable parts. How do you begin? Start by reading your Bible—not huge portions at a time, just a few verses each day. Put your Bible where you can make use of spare minutes, such as in the bathroom, or experiment until you find the perfect time slot for your quiet time. Likewise, don't expect to immerse yourself in prayer for long periods of time right away. Begin by committing each day to the Lord and simply naming each person in your family as you ask for guidance in your relationships with them.

Humor is another tool that will build stamina during times of stressful parenting. Many of your child's antics may actually be more funny when you give yourself permission to laugh.

My husband and I have a favorite comic strip that reminds us of our own family. Sharing this moment of humor is a bright spot that lifts our frame of mind, no matter what is going on around us. Sometimes seeing our own family's behavior in comic strip fashion prepares us to meet a future incident with more grace than anger.

Still another way to build stamina is through imitation. Again, just as a young athlete in training will frequently strive to emulate a successful athlete, we can look for a Christian woman we admire and let her actions be our teacher. Watch how this person acts under stress. Study her facial expressions; notice her body language.

Last of all, we build stamina for parenting by developing emotional control. While we would never want to suppress our emotions, it's important that we not allow the day-to-day events of parenting to dictate our emotions. This is not so difficult to accomplish when we realize that anger and other negative feelings at home are often attitudes brought about by society's expectations of our children's behavior. Perhaps we should consider the fact that we come into this world just as Christ would have us to be—totally free of people's imagined limitations of us, their judgments, expectations, and opinions. In the beginning we are only love; it's not until later that conflicts with our feelings emerge.

Many of these conflicts can't be avoided, but learning how to balance what others might think with what we know to be true will at least save us from *unnecessary* emotional conflicts. For example, when a child's room is in some semblance of orderly chaos, and he functions well in it, it is society's expectations that make us want him to make it into what we perceive as a clean room.

As for those conflicts that can't be avoided, proper training will leave us in good stead for those moments as well. Practice acknowledging the drama of the conflict, then letting it go. Control your breathing by taking deep breaths between positive statements, and follow it by positive actions. This doesn't mean nondiscipline—even a spanking can be positive action when done for the purpose of instruction, but it does mean acting and speaking before the conflict gets out of control.

A serious athlete trains and practices with the same intensity he gives to an important competition. For parents, the true competition begins when we release our children into the world as adults. That is when we'll find out if they make it to the finish line with glory.

Meanwhile there's training and practice every day, all day, but we don't mind. We can develop our stamina and energy to last until the end of the race.

I strain to reach the end of the race and receive the prize for which God is calling us up to heaven because of what Christ Jesus did for us.

Philippians 3:14

Father God, show me what to do with this child. Help me to lead and love. Amen.

Confession

꧁꧂

My child is in school.
Sometimes I dread picking her up.

FIVE

◦◦◦

Finding Peace Amidst Chaos

YOUR DAY HAS BEEN PERFECT. The house is clean, dinner is planned. You've even had time for a few hours of sewing and a quick jog through the park.

Or perhaps you had a great day at work. Your project was praised; everything went as planned, and you are feeling on top of the world. Now it's time to pick up your child from school or day care, and you carry a sense of optimism with you. It's going to go well today with your child. You just know it. But as your Amy or Chad or Steven or Stephanie climbs into the car, you realize the storm has begun in spite of your good intentions to keep it at bay. He is angry—his friends don't like him; his teacher is mean. Any attempt to convince him otherwise only brings a torrent of accusations aimed at you.

Once home, your child moves through the house like a tornado, leaving a trail of books, shoes, and cookie crumbs. He refuses to do his homework, hits his sister, and nags you for television privileges. You feel drained and incompetent but aren't sure why. It's not a bad day, just a typical one.

You want so badly for things to be different; you've read a million books on how to be a better mother and how to harness the good in your child. So far nothing has worked. Defeated, you find yourself dreading the end of each day as you subconsciously prepare for the storm.

What would help you most right now—this very minute?

Wouldn't it be peace?

Then let Jesus calm your storm. He can restore peace to your family just as he did for the disciples on the fishing boat so long ago. That account is one of my favorite Bible stories. It's found in Mark 4:35-41. Here, on one of his preaching journeys, Jesus and his disciples board a fishing boat on the Sea of Galilee. When an intense storm erupts, the disciples get upset when they find Jesus asleep in the stern of the boat. It is their human reaction that makes the story so appealing to real people. "Wake up!" they say. "Don't you care if we die?"

Jesus did care. The Bible tells us that he stilled the storm, and the disciples were filled with awe.

"Who is this that even the wind and sea obey?" they asked.

Today we know the answer to their question, but we sometimes forget. We forget that the God who can calm the wind and sea can calm the storms of our everyday lives. We forget that the God who stood before the raging waters and said, "Peace, be still," can act to confront the problems of modern times. We forget that the God who was, and is, and forever shall be can give us peace amidst the disruption of our lives.

Managing a challenging child is like being in the eye of a hurricane. It takes a miracle to get out, but there is no need for despair. When we call upon Jesus, he will give us inner peace within the storm. He won't always still the storm, but he will always give us the presence of mind and emotional strength to get through it.

Call for him now and listen for the still, small voice within that guides you to actions of order, patience, and serenity. This is your miracle—the calming influence of Christ upon your life. Though the struggles of rearing a disruptive child are likely to turn your household upside down again and again, the mighty strength of God will enable you and your family to stay on course and feel a sense of well-being and safety.

Then he rebuked the wind and said to the sea, "Quiet down!" And the wind fell, and there was a great calm!

Mark 4:39

A Practical Idea Sometimes a storm can be lessened by paying attention to our need for transition from one phase of activity to the next. For example, usually we subconsciously devise ways to make the transition from work to leisure. We are not even aware of how we do that until we get interrupted in some way, such as having to stop in the middle of our first cup of coffee (our transition activity) to care for an early rising, disruptive child (our interruption). Even then we may not be aware of what has gone wrong—only that something has caused the situation to become difficult and unpleasant.

If, for instance, the noise and disorder accompanying your challenging child is disruptive to your own letdown period after work, it may be helpful to find a way to hold on to your recovery time just a little longer. Perhaps your child could stay in his child care situation for an additional thirty minutes. Or maybe you could pay a teenager to serve snacks and entertain your child for a short time after you arrive home each day. It's even quite possible that your husband could be in charge of picking this child up and keeping him under tow until dinner time.

On the other hand, if you are already at home, and it's a matter of having this youngster disrupt your peace without adequate transition before moving on to dinner preparations, you can establish your own cooling down routine.

Some of the best advice my mother ever gave me was to go outside with my daughter after school. She really had in mind my daughter digging in the earth and that sort of healthful thing, but of course she doesn't live with my challenging child. It turned out that my daughter wasn't interested in focused activity and couldn't stand for me to be preoccupied with pulling weeds or raking leaves. As with many challenging children, she wanted me to be her audience and watch with bated breath as she played on the swing set.

At first I didn't like the idea of wasting time when I really wanted to be indoors starting supper, but I soon discovered that swinging helped my youngster expend energy in a positive way. Perhaps there is a pattern to the rhythm of swinging that soothes the brain as well as the spirit. At any rate, it certainly calmed her down, and it wasn't long before I learned that I could sit on the patio with a cup of tea and relax a bit myself as I watched the action.

In the winter, working with modeling clay at the kitchen table had much the same effect. Now that we home teach, we don't have quite the problem with transitions that we once had, but we still find the backyard a nice interlude between stressful activities.

Dear Jesus, I am about to drown.
Still my storm.
Amen.

Confession

᷽᷍᷍᷍

I get so angry at times that I find myself saying terrible things to my child. Things any good mother would never say.

Losing It

DO YOU HATE THE TIMES WHEN YOU LOSE IT? I mean, when you really fall out of the realm of all reason? When the muscles in your neck constrict into tight ropes and the voice coming out of your mouth belongs to the vilest, most evil witch in the kingdom?

About the only thing worse than actually throwing such a tantrum is the way we feel after it's done. Horrible. Guilty. Unworthy. Unloving. That's why it's important to remind ourselves that there's usually a reason we've behaved inappropriately. Knowing this reason can help us work on our anger and will ultimately enable us to feel better and happier about ourselves and those with whom we live.

Think for a moment about the last ranting episode you participated in. Chances are, you wanted your child to do one thing; he or she wanted to do another. And so there was arguing and bargaining and pleading and demanding, until finally your senses got overloaded and you exploded. This situation is very common in families that include a difficult child. These special children can be especially uncooperative in times of mini-crisis. They are not the kind of children for whom Mom and Dad can make an unpopular decision without repercussion.

To suggest that this time Tommy should stay home from karate or that just this once Cara could miss a dance lesson because you are not feeling well or have another important engagement does not go over well with these youngsters.

Whether it's attending special lessons or merely dragging out the arts and craft box minutes before the arrival of important company, these children will not graciously accept your "not this time." These are the children who push you beyond your better judgment, who talk you into things you haven't the time or energy to cope with. Not surprisingly, these are the times when you are apt to lose your resolve about mothering in general.

There is no cure-all for temper. We will lose it occasionally, and that's just a fact of life. But you can develop control by setting limits for yourself. If, for instance, you are too "pressed for time" because of unusual circumstances, and taking your child to a special class is creating a time stressor, admit your fallibility. Why not ask a friend to take her? Or simply say, "I'm so sorry, but I'm unable to take you to class this time because of such and such." Then get on with whatever you need to do. Though you're certain to get a lot of complaining and sulking, and maybe even a temper tantrum, you can take it because now you have at your disposal all the energy you would otherwise have used to drive the child around. This decision to set limits for yourself works the same regardless of the youngster's demands or manipulation techniques.

But what if you've already done the screaming? Now you feel guilty and ashamed about the awful things you said. "I wish I'd never had you. I hate you. You're disgusting." (Yes, I know about those ugly demons. I've been there myself.)

We are forgiven. We don't have to feel guilty and nurture the remorse in our hearts. When we lay our bad deed at God's feet, we are freed of the wrongdoing. We have let that moment go.

Here's how it works: Admit you've taken the wrong turn and are temporarily lost. Ask God to forgive you and put you back on the right path. Then, simply go forward once again. You are no longer lost. God is leading you in love. Explain this to your child. He will understand because he has the same propensity toward losing his way. But don't misunderstand the mechanics of your fallibility. Together, the two of you are certain to lose sight of God and get lost again and again. That's all right; this is a difficult journey. Just keep going forward. God is there, even when you can't see him.

The Lord is close to those whose hearts are breaking.

Psalm 34:18a

A Practical Idea Anger at your child is misdirected energy. If anger seems to well up in you too often, you may need to clarify why. If you are keeping a journal, write out your feelings after an episode of anger. Chances are, you will soon see a trend—certain situations that trigger your loss of control. Sometimes anger occurs when there is a deficiency of self-love. You know this is so when there is not enough time to yourself. Not enough rest. Not enough of the right foods. Not enough exercise. Work on correcting these deficiencies. You were important enough for God to create; you are important enough to take care of now.

At other times, anger happens because we look to our child for an improvement instead of centering our thoughts on Jesus. Whenever you find yourself in this situation, do whatever refreshes you spiritually. Perhaps that means attending church without your child. Maybe it's going for a long walk by yourself and talking to God. Sometimes it's as simple as allowing yourself to have a good cry—the kind that evolves into a tearful conversation with God. Whatever activity you choose to keep yourself both physically and spiritually healthy will usually bring about a more tolerant attitude that helps you become the loving mother your challenging child needs.

Dear God, I've lost my way. Forgive me, and put me on the right path again. Thank you. Amen.

Confession

‿❧‿

I can't let go of this child in the
normal way. People are so
judgmental I'm afraid to let
him do things on his own.

SEVEN

❧

Letting Go

SOMETIMES WE ARE DOGGED by the knowledge that our special child cannot cope with life's challenges the way the rest of us can. This can make us fearful about leaving him in what would otherwise be rather normal circumstances. We display our fear in a variety of cover-ups—hanging around the school in the guise of teacher assistant, attending birthday parties when we aren't really invited, teaching the Sunday school class under the pretense of "being called"—anything that keeps us present as a buffer for our child against the world.

Whenever we are concerned about our child's ability to function in society, we need to consult a professional who works closely with children like our own—a physician, a psychologist, or an educational specialist. Chances are, they can put our fears to rest because, as mothers, we often "see" what we fear, even when it isn't there.

Sometimes, even the assurance of a professional fails to end our worries. While the professional may equip us with data supporting his estimation of our child's ability, we are the ones who see the everyday pitfalls: the playground ostracism, the teacher's hostility, the giggles and jokes that follow our child's awkward path of activities.

Many of our child's social blunders are more upsetting to us than to him, which means we probably need to relax and happily accept his behavior as uniquely his. It may help to remember that our children are God's treasures. God is with them in a very literal sense. For within our children lies the power to bring about a full and perfect life—even without our help.

Though we may not see evidence of this ability right now, we know it's there. God has given our children every asset they need for life. This is not necessarily the same life we live, or the life we see other children living, but the very special life that God has divinely ordained for our children. As we wait to see just where this will place him or her as adults, we can be assured that within us and our children, God's wisdom and love is at work. The good we are seeking for our little boy or girl is looking for him or her right now. Such an inheritance gives us the freedom and peace of mind to know that our children can get along without us for a few hours.

> I pray that you will begin to understand how incredibly great his power is to help those who believe him.
>
> **Ephesians 1:19a**

A Practical Idea. If you're looking for the way to let go, experiment with activities until you find one or two places your child can successfully grow on his own. Bear in mind that loud, busy atmospheres are not likely to be good bets. Such environments often excite and frustrate children with learning or behavior disabilities and may lead them into situations in which they lose control. It will help if the activity is one in which your child shows unusual promise. This not only gives your child a sense of confidence but encourages the teacher to be more sensitive and tolerant toward him as well.

Surprisingly, children's church and church socials may not be the best place to leave your struggling child. This is because in the rare event that a Sunday school teacher doesn't offer understanding and support, the ensuing lessons can leave deep religious scars. (You want your youngster to experience God's love at every opportunity.) Furthermore, if socials are loud and overly rambunctious, your child may get carried away and cross the line of acceptable behavior. In either case, if you find these scenarios to be true, there is nothing wrong with staying together as a family in the main worship service of your church and waiting a while on the socials.

If you have carefully chosen a few activities for your child and are still receiving negative comments from leaders or teachers, have a few replies ready that you know by heart and can deliver with a smile. A good start might be something like this:

"But isn't he doing better! We're so proud of him, and we appreciate your loving him."

As for the negative comment, remember that there have probably been times when you've said close to the same thing about your child, so don't be too shocked or too hurt when another person does.

What if you catch your child acting inappropriately with his peers? Maybe he's acting embarrassingly silly or immature. Perhaps he's being overbearing and aggressive. You would do anything to save this dear child of yours from social failure. In fact, right now you're thinking of grabbing him and leaving before he gets labeled a "weirdo." Instead, why not carefully assess the situation? If there is an unobtrusive way to do so, take him aside and point out what you have seen and make a suggestion for change. In some instances, you may want to look for a graceful way to leave early.

Whatever happens, there's no need to feel defeated or angry at your child or yourself for having led him into a bad experience. First of all, even before you arrived on the scene, he was never alone. God was and is with your youngster wherever he is, whatever he's doing. Second, he tried, and that's what becoming is all about—being given the opportunity to interact with others and learning, albeit slowly, to make the best of it. God did plan a life of continuous growth for your child, but it isn't necessarily going to happen all at once.

Dear Father, bless this child whom you've entrusted to my care. Help me to remember that he is never without your love and wisdom. Amen.

Confession

⹌ৼ⹌

Since having this child, I've lost my
sense of self. I no longer have the
confidence to do the simplest
thing on my own.

EIGHT

❧

Rendered Incapable

DO YOU OFTEN FEEL AS IF you are losing your command on life? Do you find that responsibilities outside of family events overwhelm you to the point of defeat? I call this feeling of inadequacy a confidence deficiency. We know we have it when little things we once did with such finesse—teaching children, organizing clubs, giving dinner parties—seem larger than life. On the rare occasion when we do agree to hold a position in some organization, our job is the one that never quite gets off the ground. Certainly no one is begging us to serve another term or bragging about the sensational work we did. Meanwhile, we are constantly filled with feelings of shame and self-doubt. BSF

What's the matter? Have we really lost our ability to create, manage, and deliver? No. We have simply entered the land of the challenging child, a land where each step is rough and uncharted. Like the pioneers who had to lighten their wagon loads by throwing furniture to the prairies, we have learned to lighten our own burden by streamlining activities.

Some of this is good because when we have a disruptive child, we truly can't manage as before. We may have found that we had to surrender much of our life, including special talents and skills, just to take care of him. Doing so is one way of expressing our commitment to parenting. But there is a down side to this action. Sometimes we strip our life so bare and keep it that way so long that we forget about the wonderful God-given talents and gifts inside of us.

God doesn't ask us to surrender his gifts to us. He wills them to be released. When we withhold them, we withhold him.

I know it's hard. Advice given to other moms for finding time within the day doesn't always work for us. Often we are so tired and emotionally drained by the end of the day that there is simply nothing left.

I would not suggest that any woman wrestling with a challenging child take up a heavy agenda of activities just to prove her worth. But if you have such a child, I would urge you to continue to nurture your talents. Concentrate on one at a time. You may have put a particular skill aside for so long that you will need more training and development before you express it again. These years may be the time to sharpen and refine your abilities. Don't forget you have a guide. His name is Jesus, and when we give him our gifts, they come back to us in greater form and abundance.

Perhaps you will choose one of your gifts and really work at incorporating it into your life for a year. Or maybe you will strive to exercise ability in a different area each month. One month you will plan and give a dinner party, another month you will sew a garment, and so on. Your personal circumstances will determine your plan and the amount of progress you make. The important thing is not to lose sight of yourself as a child of God. Look beyond daily limitations and envision yourself as God does—perfectly capable in all that you do.

Talents are not to be buried beneath a stressful load; they are to be used for the glory of God and the benefit of others. So, go ahead—be happy, be fulfilled, and be free in the expression of your divine potential. Choose a confidence-building activity, and allow yourself to be supported in divine love. You can do it.

In the Old Testament God gave his people specific instruction on the use of special skills. The text, which concerns the consecration of priests in the early days, gives instructions on the sewing of their clothes. However, God's command can be applied today at a time when our talents are needed to bring glory to Christ in many different ways.

> Instruct those to whom I have given special skill as tailors to make the garments that will set him apart from others, so that he may minister to me in the priest's office.
>
> **Exodus 28:3**

(If you are a seamstress or crafter, you may want to read Exodus 28 in its entirety for a vivid account of these artfully designed garments.)

A Practical Idea If you truly want to regain former skills, make a commitment to a specific action, person, or event. Making a commitment is often the first step toward self-discovery. Once we've done this, there's no choice but to go forward with grace. Whether it's as simple as inviting someone to dinner or as impressive as starting up a home-based business, the appropriate level of commitment gives our effort a sense of direction and our end result a greater chance of success.

Dear God, you gave me gifts and abilities that you want me to use, and you gave me this child. Help me to glorify you through my talents, and to bless my child with them. Amen.

Confession

⌒⌒

But sometimes I want more out of life.
I feel angry that I have to deal
with a challenging child
instead of using my talents.

NINE

"But I Want to Do More!"

AT THE OPPOSITE EXTREME of not feeling qualified to do anything is the problem of wanting to do more but being held back by the constraints of a challenging child. One mother on public assistance, whose child has been diagnosed with a conduct disorder, explained her situation like this: "How could I possibly work when I have to be available to pick my child up from school when the principal calls and tells me they're sending her home?"

Availability plays a key role in managing a challenging child. It isn't easy for moms to find child care for such children, and when we do find it, the absence of our own parenting style often does more harm than the good we receive from being away from our child. At the end of the day, we may come home to find an out-of-control, agitated, or highly confused child who was perhaps not understood or was mistreated in our absence.

Some of us leave the work world and stay home, but not always good-naturedly. Home can be dull, or it can be frantic and chaotic. It can also be messy, disorderly, and uninspiring. Put them all together, and home can become a hot spot for depression. No wonder that in the midst of all this, our hearts pine for something more.

Perhaps we are looking at an inventory of our strengths and

abilities, and we feel angry that God has "saddled" us with a child who doesn't jive with the rest of the world. If it weren't for this child, we reason, we would be doing something important—making a difference in some meaningful way.

Occasionally, the reality of location or finance comes into the picture as well. If we must have a child like this, couldn't we live near a special school, or at the very least, our mother? And couldn't we have more money to give us better leverage in hiring child care? In bitterness, we are practically blinded with our limitations.

If life is not what we would like—if we want a more exciting call to service—the problem is not with other people in our life or the seemingly limiting environment we've been placed in. The true problem lies within our inability to accept God's abundance. If this is your present frame of mind, you may have to be reminded that you do have a boss. His name is God. All of your assignments and pay will come from him because he is the provider and the source of everything you need.

When we realize that God is our source, we don't have to resent our particular life situation. We see that God is ready to give us all that we are willing to take.

But here, at home—in the middle of nowhere, with a hard-to-manage child in the background? Yes, that challenging child is only a start, for God has a habit of using ordinary people in everyday walks of life to work on spectacular projects. As a matter of fact, once we've said yes, no power, person, or situation can stand between us and the work God wants us to do.

Just look to the Bible for proof. Women of biblical times lived under rigid social rules and regulations. The fact that there are not as many stories about women as men in the Bible may be a reflection on just how difficult it was to conquer these limitations. The important thing to notice, however, is that whenever a woman did say yes to God, he used her in a mighty way.

Here are just a few examples of Bible women whose circumstances were about as binding as any could be. As you
read about these women, you will see that God has an exciting
surprise in store for those who say yes.

Read about Sarah (Genesis 12-23). Here we will highlight
only a few portions of the story, but if you are not familiar with
the entire account, read it when you have time. Of course, if
it's already an old favorite with you, you'll be quick to agree
that Sarah teaches a myriad of lessons as her life slowly unfolds.

But Sarai and Abram had no children. So Sarai took her
maid, an Egyptian girl named Hagar, and gave her to
Abram to be his second wife.

"Since the Lord has given me no children," Sarai said,
"you may sleep with my servant girl, and her children shall
be mine."

And Abram agreed. (This took place ten years after
Abram had first arrived in the land of Canaan.) So he slept
with Hagar, and she conceived; and when she realized she
was pregnant, she became very proud and arrogant toward
her mistress Sarai.

Genesis 16:1-4

Then God did as he had promised, and Sarah became pregnant and gave Abraham a baby son in his old age, at the
time God had said; and Abraham named him Isaac (meaning "Laughter!")... (Abraham was 100 years old at that
time.)

Genesis 21:1-5

Hindsight gives us the advantage of knowing that even
though Sarah felt God had forsaken her by giving her an
unfulfilled life, she never really had to take things into her own
hands. God was going to come through all along—all she had

to do was wait patiently and lovingly. True, she was not entirely able to live up to the "lovingly" part (the Bible tells us that Sarah beat Hagar, and we can assume she probably made life miserable for the younger woman), but Sarah was nevertheless a righteous woman who allowed God to use her in his plan by always assisting Abraham in his various relocations and going along with his decisions. Sarah could have become angry and self-absorbed. Instead, she gave birth to Isaac when she was ninety years old, and she became the mother of nations.

Read about Abigail (1 Samuel 25:2-42). Again, this is a story that makes good reading in its entirety, but for expediency's sake, I will recap the plot.

David and his men were camping near the sheep ranch of Nabal and Abigail. Abigail was "a beautiful and very intelligent woman," but her husband was "uncouth, churlish, stubborn, and ill-mannered." David sent a message to the ranch asking for food and water for his men. This was not an unreasonable request, for the presence of David's men had kept the ranch safe. It was a return favor, so to speak. So, when Nabal, in his usual bad-tempered manner, refused to feed the men, David became angry and took four hundred men to the ranch for a face-to-face encounter. Meanwhile, Abigail had been informed of the situation by a servant and was laying plans for corrective action. Here is what happened:

> Then Abigail hurriedly took two hundred loaves of bread, two barrels of wine, five dressed sheep, two bushels of roasted grain, one hundred raisin cakes, and two hundred fig cakes, and packed them onto donkeys.
>
> "Go on ahead," she said to her young men, "and I will follow." But she didn't tell her husband what she was doing. As she was riding down the trail on her donkey, she met David coming towards her....
>
> When Abigail saw David, she quickly dismounted and bowed low before him.

"I accept all blame in this matter, my lord," she said. "Please listen to what I want to say. Nabal is a bad-tempered boor, but please don't pay any attention to what he said. He is a fool—just like his name means. But I didn't see the messengers you sent. Sir, since the Lord has kept you from murdering and taking vengeance into your own hands, I pray by the life of God, and by your own life too, that all your enemies shall be as cursed as Nabal is. And now, here is a present I have brought to you and your young men.

1 Samuel 25:18-27

The story goes on to tell that David assured the woman he would not kill her husband. Later, when Nabal had a stroke and died, David asked Abigail to become his wife.

So what? How does this story relate to you and me? By teaching still another lesson on living successfully under binding constraints. For Abigail had one of the most confining circumstances a godly woman can have—a bad husband. With no respectable escape from his dominant bullying, she could have spent her life feeling trapped and helpless, and no one would have blamed her. Instead, Abigail chose to rise above her situation by being faithful to God. Even when her husband did wrong, Abigail did what was right and good. Her faithfulness was rewarded at Nabal's death when she was given a new set of life circumstances, which we can only assume were much better.

If there is one thing for mothers of challenging children to gain from this story, it is the idea of being faithful to God's way even when our children and maybe our spouses are not. No matter what they say or do, we can choose to act lovingly, knowing that in doing so, we are becoming a part of the solution instead of adding to the problem.

Read about Queen Esther (Esther 1-10). This is a story of high drama in which a young Jewish girl is made Queen of

Persia. When a plan is launched to kill all the Jews in the country, Esther's older cousin, Mordecai, asks her to speak to the king on behalf of the Jews. It is a dangerous suggestion, for even though she has become a favorite in the palace, she could be put to death for requesting to speak to the king without being summoned. But Esther has said yes to God. She moves forth boldly and saves her people from death.

Esther is another woman who could have used her life circumstance as a reason for doing nothing. No one would have been surprised had she adopted an attitude of fear. Even though she was queen, her life was not secure. With no real rights or power, she could have legitimately assumed God was not going to let her do anything. Instead, she allowed God to let her be a part of his plan to save Israel.

Read about Lydia of the New Testament (Acts 16:11-15, 40). This is a short passage about a business woman who became acquainted with Paul. Paul writes this account of the meeting:

> On the Sabbath, we went a little way outside the city to a river bank where we understood some people met for prayer; and we taught the Scriptures to some women who came. One of them was Lydia, a saleswoman from Thyatira, a merchant of purple cloth. She was already a worshiper of God and, as she listened to us, the Lord opened her heart and she accepted all that Paul was saying. She was baptized along with all her household and asked us to be her guests. "If you agree that I am faithful to the Lord," she said, "come and stay at my home." And she urged us until we did.
>
> **Acts 16:13-15**

Lydia shows us again that where you are and what you are doing can't hold you back when saying yes to God's call. As a woman in New Testament days, she could have used the circumstance of having to work or simply being a woman to avoid a greater calling. Instead, she said yes to God and her home became the first church in Philippi. Her story gives credence to the importance of all women's place in the church as well.

Being the mother of a challenging child may mean that we share—with Sarah, Abigail, Esther, and Lydia—the problem of having to confront apparent limitations. Our advantage, however, is in our coming after these women. From their examples, we know that it isn't our ability God wants—only our availability for his plan for our life. When we rear a challenging child, part of this plan may be to slow down, take one day at a time, and accept the limitations our circumstances present. Once we connect with God and say yes, we can expect something important to come out of our just being here. And Sarah, Abigail, Esther, and Lydia would be pleased to know they had helped, I'm sure.

> "Who can say but that God has brought you into the palace for just such a time as this?"
>
> **Esther 4:14b**

> For God is at work within you, helping you want to obey him, and then helping you do what he wants.
>
> **Philippians 2:13**

A Practical Idea A long time ago I heard an active, successful older woman give her secret for a life of happiness and fulfillment after her retirement from public life. "Never turn down the opportunity to go anywhere or do anything," she said, "because you never know what it will lead to."

When we want a mission beyond the front door, these are true words of wisdom. As we wait for God's higher calling, we should say yes to every request for help within the realm of our restricted capabilities. It's likely that many of these opportunities will not seem matched to our special skills or talents, but the more we move into action, the easier it will be for God to have us in the right spot at the right time.

Dear God, give me the strength to make the most of what I have to offer. Amen.

Confession

※

I often wish I weren't a mother.
The job's too hard for me.

TEN

❧

"Is It Quitting Time Yet?"

IF IT'S TRUE THAT YOUR WHOLE LIFE FLASHES in front of you like a motion picture before death, I will probably not want to watch my own movie. There's too much to embarrass me. Take, for instance, the scene at the fabric store. There I am, moving quickly, almost frantically amongst the heavy cotton bolts. My youngest daughter, Alexandra, is not far behind.

"Wait, Mama," she calls out. "Wait! I know what you're trying to do. You're trying to lose me."

I find myself moving even faster—supposedly in search of the perfect color. In reality it is my daughter's childish accusation that has caused the energizing bounce to my gait. At last she catches up, but I do not welcome her with a friendly embrace. Instead, I push her aside.

"Don't hover so close to me," I say.

"Was I right?" she asks. "Was I right that you were trying to lose me?"

I shrug my shoulders and pretend to be busy examining some fabric. The loving answer is, "No." My daughter needs to hear that answer because, even though she is seven years old and should know better, television has taught her that some mothers really do abandon their families. I need to reassure her of my love—to let her see that it is always unconditional and that I will always be there for her and with her. But the word *no* doesn't come out. Stubbornly, I refuse to say it because, deep down inside, I would like very much to lose this child who has whined and fussed and thrown endless tantrums throughout the day.

End of scene. But please, God, give me a break in the final editing. At least have a subtitle that reads, "It was a very hard day."

* * * *

There are days when you want to give up. All mothers have these days, but the mother of a challenging child has them more often and with more intensity. We are the ones who fantasize about walking out the door and never coming back.

Even though such daydreams are perfectly normal, this is not a time for fantasy. This is a time for truth. Truth will ground you in strength and right thinking. Truth will carry you to success.

The truth is, we would never actually abandon our child. But we would and often do mentally withhold ourselves from him. This carries its own bag of serious consequences.

Not that we don't have good reason for our feelings. We want to remove ourselves from this child because we think that once "away," he can no longer hurt us. "Leaving," if only in the mind, would make us unavailable to his smart talk and refusal to comply. "Shutting down" would ease the discomfort of a relationship in which our child receives but never gives. "Closing off" would prevent our vulnerability to a person who drains us of every good thought. However, even mentally removing ourselves from the scene is not truly an option for the Christian mother. Children know when adults are not really with them, and experts tell us they suffer. While it's true they cannot hurt us when we are emotionally absent, neither can they reach us for nurturing or for help in sorting things out.

This time of hurt and anger is a time to let go of unhappy thoughts that carry us away from our child. Let them pass completely out of your mind. Now turn to God's truth and hold on.

God's truth is truth that will guide us in making right decisions, keeping a clear head, and maintaining emotional control as we continue on our journey. God says we are not alone. God says he will not forget us, and that we are to be strong and courageous because we will lead this child to his inheritance of peace. God does not say traveling with truth will be easy. But he does promise his protection and assures us he will lead us to a victory in his name.

> No one will be able to oppose you as long as you live, for I will be with you just as I was with Moses; I will not abandon you or fail to help you. "Be strong and brave, for you will be a successful leader of my people; and they shall conquer all the land I promised to their ancestors.... Yes, be bold and strong! Banish fear and doubt! For remember, the Lord your God is with you wherever you go."
>
> **Joshua 1:5-7, 9**

A Practical Idea When you absolutely cannot get away from your child but have hit rock bottom, eating dinner at a moderately-priced restaurant with a quiet dining room and attentive waiter can often provide just enough of a break to make things look better. Even if your child doesn't eat and spends the entire meal looking at the other customers or talking to a hostess in the lobby (within your range of vision, of course), *you* will have had the benefit of being cared for and waited on. If your family is on a tight budget, a prior agreement with your mother or a good friend, in which you swap eating at one another's home on bad days, will work just as well. Coupled with the knowledge of God's love, an evening of TLC might be all you need to get back on track.

Dear Jesus, help me in my job of mothering. Let me be emotionally present and available to my child. Amen.

Confession

❧

It's difficult to think positively
about my child.
I instinctively think the worst.

ELEVEN

❦

Nothing But
the Truth

Excerpt from a school conference:

Teacher: To be perfectly honest, Mrs. Garrison, I don't think
your daughter has a single friend in the classroom.

Me: *(silently to myself)* So the worst has been confirmed. I
half expected as much. Few invitations to parties. No
"Can I ask Susie or Ellen over?" Very little after-
school contact with other children. All of this hinted
at my child's lack of popularity. But no friends?
Absolutely no friends? This is more than I can bear.
So what do I do now, God?

WHEN NEGATIVE THOUGHTS TAKE OVER, and the future looks
hopeless or out of control, it's time to get organized. This will
not be a new concept to mothers of a special needs child. We
have been told from the onset that organization is central to
getting our child on track. According to many experts, his
room must be tidy. His school papers should be orderly. His
daily activities streamlined and systematic. But there is an area
of life we mothers can put into better order as well. I call it the
collecting of "useful" information. No one ever has much to

say about this category. Yet we moms of challenging children have a great enthusiasm for collecting facts from books, seminars, experts, lay people.

Can information ever become confusing and damaging? Yes, when its abundance and incorrect categorizing obscures our view of the truth. How readily we accept other people's opinions and statements! We are particularly influenced if the person happens to be a professional, but a neighbor or a friend can have the same effect. It doesn't seem to matter if they have only had a brief association with our child or that they don't have the whole picture; we are still willing to let these people have power over our thoughts.

I can't tell you how many times I've had my positive frame of mind shattered by some belittling remark from an outsider who doesn't know how much progress my child has made in the last month, someone who doesn't know that my child is the apple of my eye regardless of what happened on the playground or in the classroom. Nevertheless, I feel compelled to collect the unwelcome information thrust upon me, despite the fact that I know it has no merit and will only have a negative effect.

We collect hurtful information out of fear. Because we are striving so desperately to find answers, it's unrealistic to assume we will ever stop collecting. As mothers of challenging children, we must learn to judge information before we put it into our mental file. Of course, sometimes distinguishing the junk from the gems can be difficult.

One way to avoid confusion is by keeping only those items that originate with God. Because God is good, all good things come from him—health, progress, joy, happiness—all the things our children need for successful living. Good information will bring us encouragement and enlightenment. We will recognize it by its usefulness. Everything else will only tear down.

And oh, **yes**, I need to add one more thing. I learned that my daughter did have a friend, after all. So I put the former information in the round file, and for the first time I began to enjoy that "uncluttered feeling."

> God is not one who likes things to be disorderly and upset. He likes harmony.
>
> **1 Corinthians 14:33a**

A Practical Idea When everyone else is only reporting the negative about your child, you need to have a storehouse of good news on hand. Here are some special ways to stock your storehouse with nurturing information.

1. *Designate one wall in your youngster's room a wall of fame.* Hang every certificate or notice of recognition he receives, no matter how small. (If you can't put a large number of nails in your wall, a giant bulletin board can work almost as well.)

2. *Nourish your child with activities that are good for him* and that you know will bring him reports of success. Stay away from activities that are certain to frustrate him.

3. *Cultivate positive, affirming friends for the two of you,* friends who understand your child's unusual or sometimes unacceptable behavior.

4. *Always try to receive information about your child's mistakes as enlightenment,* not criticism (even if it is meant as criticism).

5. *At the end of each day, go through your child's activities and choose the best thing he did all day* to highlight his actions. If you keep a journal, record this event in glowing terms.

Dear God, clean up my heart and soul. Don't let me store anything harmful in your temple. Amen.

Confession

꙳

Good days leave me hopeful—
sometimes, too hopeful.

TWELVE

❦

Something's Going Right

TODAY IS SOMEHOW DIFFERENT. From early in the morning until late at night, your family has functioned normally and healthily. There were fewer battles to fight with your challenger. Fewer feelings of hostility. Fewer tense moments. You dare to believe this is it—the turning point you have been praying and waiting for. Maybe it is. But even if it is only a good day, and not the healing you seek for your child, you can still appreciate this break from routine and be thankful.

Without these days, we would be tempted to give up. With them, we are given a respite and the strength to go on. It's important to remember that for the mother of a challenging child, a good day is a blessing, not a promise. It does not mean that tomorrow will be the same, or that our goal has been reached. Certainly it has nothing to do with the child really being able to control his actions versus having true difficulty. However, it's an excellent day to get things done that are not usually feasible, and it's a good day to write down all the things that take place—what your family ate, where you went, what you did. Such information may be helpful in determining the right conditions for your child's progress.

Remember to thank God for today. This near perfect day was his gift of encouragement to you.

It is good to say, "Thank you" to the Lord, to sing praises to the God who is above all gods. Every morning tell him, "Thank you for your kindness," and every evening rejoice in all his faithfulness.

Psalm 92:1-2

A Practical Idea Don't let those good times just pass by; make certain you really live them. Here are a few suggestions to get you started:

1. *Visit grandparents.* Let them see the good side of your youngster.

2. *Clean out and organize your child's room.* Organize your own cabinets and cupboards, but really enjoy the "art" of it. Tie linens with pretty ribbons, stuff sachets into drawers, and put shelves into creative order.

3. *Go on a family outing* to the zoo or to a museum.

4. *Enjoy cooking meals* that require extravagant preparation.

5. *Spend time focusing on other family members* who may need your special attention.

Help me to remember this day as a sign of hope. Thank you for this gift of a grace-filled day. Thank you, God. Amen.

Confession

~ੴ~

I am often filled with the thought,
"What about me?"

THIRTEEN

"Do I Count?"

THERE COMES A TIME IN THE LIFE OF EVERY MOTHER caring for a challenging child when the demands of caregiving seem never-ending and not very fulfilling. Such days may find our minds filled with disturbing thoughts and questions. Perhaps we wonder where we fit into the overall picture of family well-being. Maybe we are questioning the value of our personhood in what seems to be a thankless, drudgery-filled calling. Maybe we have even begun to doubt God's love for us.

If any of these thoughts have ambled through your consciousness, be assured that you are not alone. Many women struggling with a challenging child will confess to having occasionally wished they'd chosen another life-path.

"If only I'd...
• stayed single.
• never had children.
• never left my career.
• never had this child."

These are not the thoughts of an evil, unloving mother. These are the thoughts of a woman feeling overworked, overburdened, and overlooked.

So, first let me reassure you that yes, dear friend, someone does care. Even if your parents are dead and your husband has left you and your best friend's not speaking to you, someone kind and wonderful cares very much about you. That someone is God, the Father Almighty. You do matter. You are the product of his idea—his kingdom on earth. He will not let you or his plans for your life fail. With him, you can turn unfortunate circumstances into victorious living. With him, there are no limitations. And all of this, simply because he is your caretaker.

Knowing that God cares for us, that our burdens can be lifted or shared, and that we are never excluded or left behind from any of God's goodness is certainly comforting and reassuring knowledge. But perhaps even more exciting is the fact that as soon as we begin to recognize our relationship with God, we become aware of the actual assets he's made available to us and are able to utilize them. We know that we are empowered to be the people we want to be and to accomplish the goals we want to reach, because we have received the most complete "care package" ever invented.

Here is what God gives us in our package:

1. **A comforter—the Holy Spirit—as our guide and counselor.**

   If you love me, obey me; and I will ask the Father and he will give you another Comforter, and he will never leave you. He is the Holy Spirit, the Spirit who leads into all truth.

   John 14:15-17

2. **Protection.**
   Bad things may happen to us, but as Christians we know that God's presence watches over us, helping us turn bad into good. There is no need for us to fear tomorrow when our trust lies in the security and safety of an eternal future with Christ.

We live within the shadow of the Almighty, sheltered by the God who is above all gods. This I declare, that he alone is my refuge, my place of safety; he is my God, and I am trusting him. For he rescues you from every trap, and protects you from the fatal plague. He will shield you with his wings! They will shelter you. His faithful promises are your armor. Now you don't need to be afraid of the dark any more, nor fear the dangers of the day; nor dread the plagues of darkness, nor disasters in the morning. Though a thousand fall at my side, though ten thousand are dying around me, the evil will not touch me. I will see how the wicked are punished but I will not share it. For Jehovah is my refuge! I choose the God above all gods to shelter me. How then can evil overtake me or any plague come near? For he orders his angels to protect you wherever you go. They will steady you with their hands to keep you from stumbling against the rocks on the trail. You can safely meet a lion or step on poisonous snakes, yes, even trample them beneath your feet! For the Lord says, *"Because he loves me, I will rescue him; I will make him great because he trusts in my name. When he calls on me I will answer; I will be with him in trouble, and rescue him and honor him. I will satisfy him with a full life and give him my salvation." * *For a powerful reminder of God's love, replace the word* he *from this point on with the pronoun* you *and read out loud. Here's how it would read:*

Because you love me, I will rescue you; I will make you great because you trust in my name. When you call on me I will answer; I will be with you in trouble, and rescue you and honor you. I will satisfy you with a full life and give you my salvation.

Psalm 91

3. **Abundance.**
As we use the ideas given to us by the Holy Spirit, we are
led to situations of plenty.

Jesus said to the disciples, "If you only have faith in God—
this is the absolute truth—you can say to this Mount of
Olives, 'Rise up and fall into the Mediterranean,' and your
command will be obeyed. All that's required is that you
really believe and have no doubt! Listen to me! You can
pray for *anything,* and if you believe, you have it; it's
yours!

Mark 11:22-24

4. **Peace of mind and heart.**
The light of Christ illumines every area of life with his love
and peace. We know that regardless of what we might be
going through today, God's love can guide us toward
decisions and actions that generate a feeling of confidence
and peace.

I am leaving you with a gift—peace of mind and heart! And
the peace I give isn't fragile like the peace the world gives.
So don't be troubled or afraid.

John 14:27

A Practical Idea Here are a few things you can do that will
result in better feelings about your life in general.

- *Join a support group*—there is a group for almost every syn-
drome or problem on earth. Even if you are shy and not
likely to speak up, you'll soon find that just knowing other
people have the same problems as you will make you feel
better.

- *Find good psychological and medical counsel.* You might begin the search by asking other parents of challenging children for recommendations. If you attend a support group, you will probably have an opportunity to meet many of these professionals when they speak at your meetings. Look for someone who understands your child's problem, someone whom you and your child both like and feel comfortable with, and someone who seems to genuinely like your child. Also, because so many behavior disorders are just now being earnestly researched, your counselors need to possess a willingness to learn.

  Don't assume, however, that the answer is undoubtedly with professional helpers. Jesus is still our best counselor, and his services are free.

  For unto us a Child is born; unto us a Son is given; and the government shall be upon his shoulder. These will be his royal titles: "Wonderful," "Counselor," "The Mighty God," "The Everlasting Father," "The Prince of Peace."
  Isaiah 9:6

- *Write yourself a letter of praise and encouragement,* telling yourself all the things you need to hear. Place it in your Bible and read it six months from the date you write it. (Be sure to mark this date on your calendar.)

  Very often, a small dose of self-care can give us a brighter, happier perspective on life.

  Dear heavenly Father, let me feel your love. Help me to see your loving provision for me in your word and the people you put in my life. Amen.

Confession

❧

I don't have enough faith that
God can heal my child.

FOURTEEN

Strong Medicine for the Weak in Faith

NOT ENOUGH FAITH to bring about a miracle for your child? Nonsense. I am almost certain you have more faith than you realize. For instance, every time you go to bed and fall asleep you exercise faith. Think about it; to be willing to lapse into nothingness with the assurance that in a few hours we'll awake has got to be a major step in trusting a greater power. At the very least, it's a starting place for building the real thing. This is not to say, however, that deep faith just happens. It doesn't. Strong, abiding faith is acquired.

Even so, not all people—not even all Christians—will ever truly possess it. Why is this? Perhaps because deep faith calls for total surrender, an act most humans don't want to do. To surrender means relinquishing our attempts at controlling life. It's admitting that even though we've been fighting the battle with everything we've got, we don't have enough.

But to surrender is to take the most important step in the problem-solving process because this is when faith is born, and it is at this moment we feel the burden of "fixing things ourselves" lifted from our shoulders.

The mother of a challenging child should seek this kind of faith, if for no other reason than the peace she gains. Surely nothing provides a greater sense of peace and security than allowing God to love us and building our life on that rich, deep love. This is in essence the definition of faith, and this is all you will need for the rearing of your child.

How does one develop such faith? Why not start where you are right now? Begin this minute by acknowledging the faith you do have and giving thanks for it. Recall every time you have scored a faith victory. Perhaps one time will be the moment when you first came to know Christ as your personal Savior. Perhaps another time will be when you relied on God to pull you through a financial crisis. Maybe it was when you depended on God to grant you a particular desire or longing. Write these victories down and read them aloud.

Next, designate a time to pray for your child each day. Make copies of your child's picture and distribute them among friends you have asked to join you in prayer. Ask them to place the picture in their Bibles where it will be a reminder of your need.

Prayer is not only a faith builder; it is also a vital link in the overall process of restoration and renewal. Read Mark 9:17-29. This is the story of the healing of a boy with an evil spirit. The disciples tried to call out the spirit but were unable to. After Jesus had successfully done so, they asked him why they had not been able to call out the spirit.

Jesus replied, "Cases like this require prayer."

Mark 9:29

Couple your prayer with Bible reading. When we read God's Word, we become sensitive to his will. We seem to have an inner guide leading us to right choices and decisions. Sometimes a particular verse will speak to us in a specific way. This is not "reading" things into Scripture. It is using the Bible as it was intended to be used.

And don't overlook the importance of church attendance.

When we are building our faith, the church is a logical place to begin. It helps us act out corporately what we may not be able to do by ourselves. Besides, there is strength in numbers.

> For where two or three gather together because they are mine, I will be right there among them.
>
> **Matthew 18:20**

Another good activity for this time of faith building is to creatively express your growing faith through the arts. Write poetry, do needlepoint or paint a picture conveying some aspect of your deepening faith. The finished product can be a visible testimony of your faith in God, and the whole family can benefit from it.

A strong faith in God's love for our challenging child is very important, for faith assures us this child is in God's care and will one day lead a meaningful life. It is not important what church we go to or even how often we go. In fact, there is no biblical evidence that faith was ever reserved for the extremely righteous. Jesus gave his love and care to those who asked for it. Read these stories about people in need:

> Luke 18:35-43 (A blind beggar receives his sight.)
> Luke 17:11-19 (Ten men are healed of leprosy.)

In both stories you will discover there is no mention of the people's religious standing. They simply believed.

As incredible as it sounds, the same holds true for you. Your child's future is taken care of the moment you believe.

> What is faith? It is the confident assurance that something we want is going to happen. It is the certainty that what we hope for is waiting for us, even though we cannot see it up ahead.
>
> **Hebrews 11:1**

A Practical Idea If you fear you don't have enough faith that God can give your child a joyful and meaningful life, don't waste time worrying about the amount of faith. For now, just choose to believe as much as you can. Jesus said even a little faith is enough to work wonders.

However, don't forget that faith needs to be followed by action that demonstrates what we believe. Remember the story of the woman who touched the hem of Jesus' robe and was healed? (Mk 5:25-34). Recall that first she believed, then she made the actual effort to go to Jesus, and finally she carried through with the action she believed. The Bible says that as soon as she touched Jesus she knew she was well.

When we believe God can help our children reach their unique potential, we are to ask God for help and then act as if we know he has given it.

How easy it is to get into the habit of referring to our children as difficult, slow, or maybe even disabled. Certainly there are going to be situations or days when it doesn't seem as if they have improved, but these times can almost always be attributed to our own human shortcomings. Lack of sleep, improper diet, and too much stimulation either on our part or the child's are all things that can cause a challenging child's behavior to deteriorate. When this happens, we just have to keep remembering that with God nothing is impossible.

For if you had faith even as small as a tiny mustard seed you could say to this mountain, "Move!" and it would go far away. Nothing would be impossible.

Matthew 17:20b

Dear God, give me deep, abiding faith upon which to build miracles. Thank you. Amen.

Confession

❦

This child can make me so angry
that I fear I may hurt him.

FIFTEEN

Win, Win, Win

WOULDN'T IT BE NICE TO WIN one of the battles now and then? To get in there with the latest discipline technique and stick it out until it works? The truth is, if you fight against your challenging child when he's angry, there is no winning because at this moment the child is beyond all reason. Chances are good he won't respond as the books predict, which will only make you angrier.

Oh, yes, I do know how it feels to be sassed by a child in public, to have her stand before you and defiantly refuse to obey. I understand the frustration of purchasing every parenting book on the market with no return of success. I, too, have read my Bible and raised the rod to no avail—except for my body heat getting hotter and hotter.

This is the point at which I try focusing on a God thought. I think of a phrase or Scripture that is easy to remember and especially meaningful. I repeat it over and over throughout the moment of tension. Surprisingly, I find that I cannot concentrate on my anger and on God at the same time. Soon the moment of anger passes and I'm free to handle my child in an appropriate "grown-up" fashion.

Want to give it a try? Here are a few God thoughts to get you started:

- *God loves my child and he loves me.*

- *God can give me the patience and strength I need right now.*

- *God is guiding me now.*

- *God is with me.*

A Practical Idea Make a list of peace-generating ideas, and hang them on your refrigerator to refer to in a moment of crisis. With practice, the reaction or lack of reaction you desire will come more easily. Here are a few that work for me:

1. *Be aware of your anger as it first begins.* As you feel your muscles tighten or your breathing become heavier, have a predetermined signal ready that tells you to take positive action rather than go forward with the mood. This might be crossing and uncrossing your fingers or rubbing your head—any silly little action that will cause you to stop, think, and take positive action.

2. *Proceed with a positive action such as separating yourself from your child.* Instead of sending your child on time out, give yourself a time out behind closed doors. Walk around the room a couple of times, breathe deeply, or lie down.

3. *Share a predetermined signal with your child that says, "Stop."* This could be a raised hand or a particular look—used sparingly, your child knows you mean business.

4. *Let go of the need to control everything and everybody.* You will feel better all the way around.

A sense of failure usually follows a mother's angry outburst at her challenging child. We tend to view our lack of control as some kind of evil misdeed that will be heavily imprinted upon our child's memory bank. In truth, most of our youngsters have poor short-term memories and will drop the incident in record time and pick up with whatever they were doing prior to your anger. It is this very vulnerability that makes it so important for us to put forth an enormous effort to stop trying to control ourselves and let God do the controlling. When we are drawing upon his love, we will find ourselves winning more and more often without even going to battle.

Fix your thoughts on what is true and good and right. Think about things that are pure and lovely, and dwell on the fine, good things in others. Think about all you can praise God for and be glad about.

Philippians 4:8b

Dear Father, fill me with peace at this moment of anger. Soothe my feelings with loving thoughts. Amen.

Confession

~~✄~~

My feelings are easily hurt.
Criticism of my child or my
parenting style brings me
close to tears.

SIXTEEN

~~·❧·~~

A Mother's Tears

ONE DAY WE WERE VISITING WITH MY PARENTS when our challenging daughter proceeded to skate her way through the living room. I gently told her to take the skates off, but a few minutes later she skated through again on her way out. By this time, we were all deep in conversation, and our daughter was outdoors before an appropriate pause surfaced. My mother looked at me and chided, "Now, that's exactly what's wrong. You never make her do anything."

I can't remember what followed except that I was soon dabbing at my tears with a tissue. There was so much more to my life than what my mother could see in that one instance. Months and months of consistency, of being on behavior modification programs, attending counseling, visiting doctors, administering medication, and you name it. But the fact that I hadn't seen the sense in disturbing a once-a-year visit with an unpleasant scene was, in my mother's opinion, a parenting flaw worth commenting on.

Now let me say that there is no one more loving than my mother, and I would like to set the record straight by making it clear she later apologized and assured me she hadn't understood the situation. However, I did want to use my story to illustrate how it's often the wonderful, well-meaning people who hurt us with criticisms of our child or our parenting skills.

Most of the time their comments are not really so terrible, but they hurt us because we feel that in some vague way they show disapproval or our unworthiness. When the criticism comes from a family member, all kinds of buried feelings rise to the forefront: "I never measured up." "You liked her better than me." "I never felt loved."

Jesus had a special place in his heart for people who were criticized; he saw the effort behind the criticized action. The famous blessing of the children in Matthew 19:13-15 was born out of the disciples' criticism of the mothers who brought their children to Jesus. As you read this passage you'll notice that Jesus first restored the mother's dignity by having the children come forward.

But Jesus said, "Let the little children come to me, and don't prevent them."

Matthew 19:14a

Then he taught a lesson about the need to have a childlike trust in God.

For of such is the Kingdom of Heaven.

Matthew 19:14b

Jesus follows a similar pattern in Mark 14:3-9 when a young woman with a bad reputation anointed his head with oil. The other dinner guests at the table were indignant about the waste and began criticizing the woman for spending money on perfume instead of giving it to a worthy cause. Jesus put a stop to the criticism by defending the woman's action. Then he taught a lesson about worship:

You always have the poor among you, and they badly need your help, and you can aid them whenever you want to; but I won't be here much longer. She has done what she could, and has anointed my body ahead of time for burial. And I tell you this in solemn truth, that wherever the Good News is preached throughout the world, this woman's deed will be remembered and praised.

Mark 14:7-9

Today, Jesus isn't here in person to defend us against harsh and sometimes unfair judgments, but he will still use the situation to teach a lesson if we will let him. You may have heard that when we mull over a person's criticism, we allow that person to have power over us. Since we know that God often speaks to us through another person, consider the fact that he may be using the very person who criticizes you as a type of spiritual teacher for your personal development. Now, instead of getting hurt or angry at this person, we can almost feel grateful.

There are so many different ways to do things and so much about life we have yet to learn. Be honest with your appraisal of the criticized action. If what you are doing isn't working and you need some advice, try something new. Your critical appraiser places you in the invigorating atmosphere of the classroom and offers an opportunity to learn and grow. Don't feel intimidated or punished by a few harsh words. Lessons are a time for experimentation, exploration, investigation, and introspection. When we think we have the only right way, we deprive ourselves of these exciting learning experiences.

Most of us will probably discover that some criticisms lead to meaningful change, while others seem to have no effect on our life whatsoever. When we can see beyond the hurt of the moment, the Holy Spirit will use each incident to guide us to the right conclusion.

Jesus doesn't want us to be hurt and wounded by others, and yet he knew we would be—over and over again because we live in an imperfect world. But in spite of the inevitable struggles we'll face throughout life, and the unkindness and evil we're sure to encounter, we know we are not alone. Jesus promises to be with us and reassures us that the victory is his. He encourages us to smile. With such knowledge we can take criticism with the heartfelt gratitude of love.

Here on earth you will have many trials and sorrows; but cheer up, for I have overcome the world.

John 16:33b

A Practical Idea When people criticize you, don't react in haste. Listen to what they have said and have a ready reply. People rarely continue to tear down when we give them a kind, loving answer that shows respect for their opinion and appreciation for their concern. We can't possibly listen for the lesson if we are reacting in anger. Here are a few examples that might help you with a loving answer:

"I'm disappointed that you feel that way, but I'm glad you want to help."

"I'm sorry you feel that way." Then to yourself you may add, "But I like it the way I'm doing it."

Or, say nothing at all out loud, while to yourself you reply, "I don't like what I'm hearing, but it doesn't hurt me or my child to listen."

Dear Jesus, it hurts when people criticize me or my child. Please heal the hurt quickly so that I can go on to learn the lesson. Amen.

Confession

~~❧~~

Today was so bad
I don't think
I can go on.

SEVENTEEN

 ❦

Tomorrow Will Be Better

ONCE IN A WHILE THERE WILL BE A DAY SO BAD you won't believe you are going to make it through. Of course you will, you know. In fact, chances are good that you will not only make it to the end of this day, but that you will live to see the dawning of tomorrow—a decidedly promising improvement over today's present situation in which you are feeling overwhelmed, stressed out, or just very tired.

Such feelings are common to the mother of a challenging child, but when experienced for long periods of time, as most of us do experience them, these emotions can cause us to suffer sadness and depression. We may feel trapped, victimized, and hopeless. Sometimes we may think the question is not *if* we can go on, but whether or not we *want* to go on—and we are pretty sure we don't want to.

Because these feelings are not healthy either for us or our children, it is a wise mother who takes preventive measures against the problems that can cause such despair. Not surprisingly, bad-day prevention, like most preventive action, takes place before the day begins. If you are reading this at the end of a particularly trying day, affirm your self-worth by reminding yourself that you are a good mother, coping on the level God has placed you for now. Then take heart in the truth that tomorrow can be better. No matter how far we fall from our parenting goals, no matter how deep the level of our despair, we know that we can always start over by simply deciding to.

Here are a few ideas for starting a new day with hope:

- **Start the new day by returning it to God.**

When we give up on the idea of controlling our life, the enormous pressure for success is lifted. Perhaps this is because by surrendering to Christ we are able to follow his course of action instead of our own. We know that regardless of how little we accomplish, or how many mistakes we make throughout the day, we are in the right place doing the right thing because we are where Christ wants us. While the way may not always be clear, we are confident and at peace because we are following his plan.

As you prepare for this new day, make plans to do the things you already know God wants you to do. Be prepared for unexpected twists and turns and maybe a few bumps and jostles as you set forth on your new adventure. Such mishaps are nothing to be afraid of—nothing to be discouraged from. God knows exactly what lies ahead, and you are in his hands.

You saw me before I was born and scheduled each day of my life before I began to breathe. Everyday was recorded in your Book!

Psalm 139:16

- **Start the new day with renewed strength.**

God promises us the strength we need to get through the day. However, a particularly bad day calls for an early bedtime for both you and your child. If you are reading this before supper, plan an especially nourishing meal. A menu of chicken breasts, baked potatoes, salad, bran muffins, and a glass of juice makes a simple but satisfying meal that will help restore your energy and please your family at the same time.

When you awaken the next day, feeling refreshed, give yourself some exercise time. Because others have already said so much about the importance of exercise for staying physically fit, I will only remind you that it can also help increase physical strength.

For I can do everything God asks me to do with the help of Christ who gives me the strength and power.

Philippians 4:13

- **Start the new day without looking back.**

    Leave yesterday and its problems behind you. Reliving ugly scenes in your mind will only reinforce the problem. Replace such thoughts with the visual image of you, your child, and Jesus doing something fun together.

Create in me a new, clean heart, O God, filled with clean thoughts and right desires.

Psalm 51:10

- **Start the new day with an attitude of thanksgiving.**

    The miracle is the fact that it is a new day. Its very existence is evidence that God loves you and believes in you. Whatever your particular mission in life (and surely it has something to do with raising this special child), God is giving you another day to show your love for him through obedience.

See how very much our heavenly Father loves us, for he allows us to be called his children—think of it—and we really are!

1 John 3:1

- **Meet the new day filled with a spirit of divine love.**

Awaken with determination to express this love in every thought, word, and action. As you and your child begin to see each other through the eyes of love, harmony will be restored to your soul and your homelife as well.

Live within my love.

John 15:9b

A Practical Idea Whenever you experience emotional and physical overload, free yourself from whatever you can. Sure, there are certain things you can't get out of—preparing supper, getting older children off to school, and doing the laundry. But if you'll think about it for a minute or two, you might be surprised at the number of things you don't have to do.

You-Don't-Have-To's:

1. *You don't have to answer the phone.* (Especially not when you own an answering machine.)

2. *You don't have to hold on when waiting for someone on the telephone.* (Just try again later.)

3. *You don't have to answer the door.* (But to avoid worrying people, you could leave a note on the door saying that you can't be interrupted at the time.)

4. *You don't have to read or even open junk mail.*

5. *You don't have to keep a tidy house.* (Though it will help your already weakened morale.)

6. *You don't have to have the television on.* (Except maybe if your husband is watching after a long day at work.)

7. *You don't have to serve dessert.* (Some families save it for weekend meals and then offer it as a reward for the completion of chores.)

8. *You don't have to get upset* just because your challenging child or everyone else in the household is unhappy. You can be calm.

Thankfully, God doesn't greet us each morning with a long list of expectations. He asks only that we begin the day in an attitude of love. When we can do this, the reward is great, for our decision to love can soften the bite of a difficult relationship or brighten the heart of a drudgery filled soul. Once we've discovered that the secret of living with adversity or overcoming despair lies in the act of loving one another, our lives are well on the way to improvement, and we know the new day is going to be all right.

Dear God, help me to start over again. Amen.

Confession

❧

I lose hope when my
child regresses.

EIGHTEEN

~~✖~~

Two Steps Forward, Three Steps Back

THE PROGRESS OF A CHALLENGING CHILD IS BITTERSWEET. We know that for every victory there is another battle up ahead. Sometimes the disappointment is overwhelming.

See if this sounds familiar:

Things are going reasonably well. The medication is being tolerated, academic success is experienced, and the behavior of our child has remarkably improved. My husband and I are pleased beyond words. Then for no apparent reason the bottom falls out. Nothing works anymore. None of the little tricks from my bookshelf, none of the tiny pills from the pharmacy, none of the emergency back-up plans from friends and relatives do their "thing." My husband and I don't know what to think. We don't even know what has happened, but we agree it feels like something akin to being hit by a truck.

Exactly what has happened? Simply this. Something fell short of our expectations. The child, the medicine, or our own parenting skills didn't measure up to expected performance.

Certainly, "off" days are fairly common in the lives of our challenging children, but signs of reversal can have a more threatening effect upon our parental psyche than an ordinary bad day. Reversals create a tendency within us to believe we've lost all the headway made—that our child's case is hopeless— that we ourselves will never make it through.

At such times, it's important to remind ourselves that a

reversal is only temporary. Illness, great excitement created by upcoming holidays, house guests, or trips away from home can all cause a challenging child to regress to old ways. It seems to always happen at those times when we want our youngster to act like a normal child or at least be reasonably good. No wonder we feel defeated. No wonder we feel the need to be comforted and reassured that the lost progress will soon be regained. For of course past experience can almost always point to the fact that things will soon be back to whatever is considered normal for our households.

In the meantime, many of us have found that it helps to be good to yourself. Accept that you are making progress each day no matter what happens, and that you and your child are capable of doing all that is required of you. Love yourself unconditionally, just as you love your child. Look beyond this setback to see things as God does. God sees your child as made in his image. Can anything be more perfect and wonderful?

> He created everything there is—nothing exists that he didn't make. Eternal life is in him, and this life gives light to all mankind.
>
> **John 1:3-4**

> Then God looked over all that he had made, and it was excellent in every way.
>
> **Genesis 1:31a**

A Practical Idea Sometimes the best thing to do when we seem to have lost ground with our challenging child is to think back to earlier times—maybe as far back as a year or two. Usually when we do this we see that we've made and maintained progress to some degree. While this may seem like obvious and simple advice, it's amazing how shortsighted we get during rough phases.

Father God, when I feel myself sliding down, remind me that I have only to pick myself up and climb the ladder in order to reach the top again. Amen.

Confession

❦

I hate the way my child gets the
best of me and drags me
down even when
I want to be happy.

NINETEEN

❦

Bad-Day Blues

IT'S EASY TO RESENT A CHILD WHO RUINS THE DAY. You feel helpless about how to feel and behave because no matter how happy or determined you set out to be, this child will soon pull you down into the bottomless pit.

Fortunately, we can possess peace and happiness in spite of all that is going on around us because we are a part of God's kingdom. "For the Kingdom of God is within you" (Lk 17:21b).

God has empowered us to create a mental climate that exemplifies his kingdom through harmonious, happy, and loving thoughts. This is important because nothing can destroy the peace of a household faster than the anger of a challenging child transmitted to his mother and then, through her, to the rest of the family.

Instead of allowing your challenging child to tear down family morale, use your influence to build positive attitudes in the midst of daily struggles. A good way to stay upbeat is to give positive nurturing to everyone (not just family members) we encounter throughout the day. It is Christ who gives us the best examples on how to do this. If you have time, follow him through the gospels as he teaches, heals, and shares his love. You will notice that as Jesus traveled about the countryside, he frequently improved people's mental climate by filling them with love, hope, and peace of mind.

One of my favorite New Testament stories is that of the woman Jesus met at the well in the village of Sychar (see John 4:1-45). The woman had been divorced five times in a society that looked on even one divorce as unacceptable. Furthermore, she was now living with a man not her husband. Surely life cannot have been easy for her. She was probably looked down on by other women and must have felt friendless, lonely, and unhappy. A few of her remarks indicate she was probably a negative person. And yet Jesus was able to lift her out of despair and show her hope. This is what he does over and over again throughout the New Testament—meet people where they are and lift them higher. This is what the mother of a challenging child must do, too.

Where to begin? With what you have. Don't worry about changing the child. Yes, he is a powerhouse of emotions and actions that easily overwhelm his more reticent parents, but some of these volatile emotions are admirable. No one is more enthusiastic at the start of a new adventure. No one is friendlier and more outgoing with strangers. No one can be as sensitive toward others' feelings in a moment of crisis. No one is more creative or more charming during his good moments. So harness the good points, and accept this child as he is right now—because that is what you have right now.

Next, choose to be happy at the start of each day. Through our senses, intellect, and imagination, we have the ability to create our own world. Though it is not always easy to stay clear of negativity, we do own the power to stand firm in happiness. We do this by learning to balance caring for others with caring for ourselves. Here are a few ways to do this:

1. **Make a list of all the good things in your life,** and read it aloud every morning as soon as you get up. As a variation of this idea, you could make a list of the positive side of your child's emotions to help you see and appreciate the "flip side" of your youngster.

2. **Focus on the promises of Scripture.** Make or purchase Scripture cards, and put them in strategic places where you'll be sure to see them throughout the house.

3. **Try playing beautiful, inspirational music** early in the morning as children prepare for school. It can have a soothing effect on anxious minds.

4. **Remember, you are not your child.** He is his own little person with individual traits and behavior. You may wish he were more like you, but did you ever consider that he may be wishing for a mother more like himself? As you look for the good in your youngster, you'll become acutely aware of the lessons he brings you. Lessons on loving... on waiting... on giving. Indeed, living with this child is an unsurpassed lesson in spiritual harmony.

Stop thinking of your child's negative responses to life as bad behavior. Think of it as a request to stop his pain. Interpret his belligerent outbreaks into the language of love. Visualize him saying, "Mom, create my joy."

Wouldn't you do it?

I'm betting the answer is yes. You would give him the moon if it would make things better, which is why it's so important that you not let this child pull you down. You can't help him climb out of his turmoil if you are there, too.

Rest assured that change will come to this child. It will come when he realizes how unfairly he is using people. It will come when the timing is right. But until then, it is all right for you to feel good even when he is obviously miserable. His unhappiness is just a type of growing pain.

Sometimes we can halt our challenging child's bad mood or at least keep ourselves from joining him in the doldrums by spontaneously picking up an activity or special interest. Here are a few activities that have often helped me establish a more pleasant mental atmosphere:

1. **Make a surprise care package for someone on a limited income.** Preparing a surprise for another person always puts a note of gaiety in the air, which may in turn actually improve your challenging child's mood. Hard candy, hand lotion, note pads, and pens are some of the inexpensive items you could include.

2. **Serve a food item normally passed up at the grocery store because of its impracticality or cost.** When I was a child, my family never bought the tiny, select-your-own-cereal packages, so on the rare occasion that I place one of these on my own breakfast table, I still experience a rush of childish delight at the prospect of starting the day with so many choices. However, if you were to do this or something similar and your challenging child gets confused by the choices, you may have to position his selection in such a way that he *thinks* he has made his own decision.

3. **Find a simple art project you can enjoy in the presence of your challenging child.** For me, it's decoupage. I can spend hours cutting out pictures and gluing them onto an object. My obvious interest in what I'm doing almost always attracts my daughter, who is soon happily putting a bad mood aside to have fun with me.

Actually, being happy in spite of our circumstances is not as hard as we all want to make it. For me, a great eye-opener was realizing that the only moment we have to be happy is now—this very moment. Yesterday is gone; tomorrow isn't here yet. All we have is this place in time right now. I like this concept because it's both realistic and manageable. When we are handling the present in a way we can be proud of, the future can't help but look promising.

A Practical Idea Make a *Name-Your-Day* book for both you and your child. (See Appendix B.)

Dear God, grant me happiness and the ability to enjoy life without guilt. Amen.

Confession

❧

Parenting is too hard for me.
I don't know what to do
with my challenging child.

TWENTY
~•❧•~

It's a Tough Job...
and I Have to Do It

REARING CHILDREN IS A DIFFICULT JOB no matter the circumstance, but meeting the needs of a special child adds yet another element of concern to the parenting role. You are filled with questions: Is there something wrong with my child? Or is he simply willful? Do we seek professional help, or do we try to manage awhile on our own? What about the other children? What should I expect from them during this time of family crisis? Is it fair to concentrate on this one child? What about my own performance? Is something I'm doing causing the problem? These are only a few of the questions that may torment the mother of a troubled child.

If she is facing the problem alone as a single parent or because her spouse is disinterested, she can feel especially burdened. This doesn't mean that a woman with ample emotional support from others is without doubts and fears. All of us share the deep dark secret that maybe, just maybe, we aren't a good enough parent. Maybe our challenging child is proof.

So, here is good news to all whose minds are filled with questions and who wrestle with doubts of capability. Someone has the answers to your questions. Someone has the time and know-how to teach you all you need to know about nurturing a challenging child. Someone can help you become the perfect parent.

Oh, yes, I know what you're doing at this moment. You are probably squinting your eyes in disbelief and asking, "Who on God's earth would do all of that for me?" And I can only assume that deep down inside you have already guessed the answer is God himself.

Perhaps now you are angry. Maybe you're feeling that God has let you down with the struggles of this child. Maybe you're wondering how you can believe he will be the source of your help. Maybe you think this book has taken on a syrupy, sanguine tone. If so, bear with me. Even though your heart may be hardened with disappointment, and your opinion of spiritual guidance not high, you can take your Bible off the shelf and study it from a historical perspective. Spend a few minutes browsing through it. From a strictly factual point of view, I think you'll be amazed at the clear evidence of God's presence as a parenting mentor. For if there have been easier times than today to raise children, there have also been more difficult times. And God was always there.

Remember the story of Moses? (See Exodus 1, 2:1-10.) Imagine the horror of putting your baby boy afloat in the Nile River to keep him from being slaughtered. In a similar incident, Mary and Joseph heeded the warning of an angel and rose in the night to carry the infant Jesus to Egypt, where he would escape Herod's senseless execution of baby boys (See Matthew 2:13-23). In both cases, these parents were divinely guided to the right action. And it is this same divine presence that will guide us in meeting the needs of our own children.

Each of us has the capability of becoming the perfect parent. We begin by the simple act of following our role model, for each of us has the perfect parent no matter the faults of our birth parents. This perfect parent is Christ, who never favors one child above another. He is always just, always wise, and never withholds his love. Incredible as it sounds, this wisdom and tenderness is available to human parents as well.

Parenting will always be the greatest challenge. But God has given us every skill and all the knowledge we need to do it well. There is, however, the little matter of putting our children in his hands while we wait for wisdom to fall upon us. Though it is often hard to believe, it is just at this point that wisdom seems to break through. Perhaps the first hint of this knowledge is when we become aware that God will not let us down in the rearing of this child. For this child who can read like an adult but can't learn math, who is musically talented but can't play ball, who can communicate with adults but can't make a friend his own age, who is a bundle of disruptive energy but a blanket of love—this child who by outward appearances is a moving mass of contradictions—was created by God. So, thankfully, we need never fear that God will leave us on our own to raise this child. This youngster is one of God's priceless treasures—a divine masterpiece. For this child, God moves us to claim our heritage of wisdom just at the moment we need it most. That moment can be right now.

A Practical Idea Throughout the Bible we see that God uses the love in a parent-child relationship to teach man about God's love. Obviously, God sees love as the single most important element in parenting.

> The Father loves this man because he is his Son, and God has given him everything there is.
>
> **John 3:35**

> For God loved the world so much that he gave his only Son so that anyone who believes in him shall not perish but have eternal life.
>
> **John 3:16**

God's solution to the problems of life was love. So we know that if we want to be godly parents, we must be loving parents who practice the art of unconditional love. Of course there is no question that the unattractive behavior of your challenging child makes him seem less lovable at times. You ask your child to do one thing; he stubbornly does another. Perhaps he destroys property or insults you in public or blatantly lies. As you look at him you are not seeing the adorable infant once placed in your arms as a newborn whom you vowed you would love with all your heart for ever and ever. You are seeing an incorrigible, manipulating brat who doesn't appear to know the first thing about love. And yet, God has asked you to love him—to be a loving parent. Could it possibly work today and with this child, you ask.

Yes, your child will learn the meaning of love from you as you put into action the truths you learn from the Bible. A good place to start is 1 Corinthians 13. This chapter of the Bible is known among Christians as the love chapter and is frequently read at weddings as a challenge to young couples. But just look at what a complete guide this Scripture can be to the mother of a challenging child. Here is a portion of the passage:

> Love is very patient and kind, never jealous or envious, never boastful or proud, never haughty or selfish or rude. Love does not demand its own way. It is not irritable or touchy. It does not hold grudges and will hardly even notice when others do it wrong. It is never glad about injustice, but rejoices whenever truth wins out. If you love someone you will be loyal to him no matter what the cost. You will always believe in him, always expect the best of him, and always stand your ground in defending him.
>
> 1 Corinthians 13:4-7

. Taken thought by thought, we begin to see strong implications for its use in our daily lives. Here is how I use it in my own life:

- **Love is very patient and kind.**
When my child's lack of self-control causes me to become impatient and unkind, it is the remembrance of God's love for me that helps me try again. I know that my behavior should not be dependent upon my child's because kind love does not expect any return.

- **Love is never jealous or envious.**
When I look at my sister's perfectly behaved children, whose obedience is indeed worn like a crown on her head, this part of the Scripture reminds me that jealousy is not appropriate. Christ's love for me reminds me that I would not really trade my highly imaginative but sometimes unmanageable child for anyone else's. Generous love is love that can be happy for other people's easier parenting journey.

- **Love is never boastful or proud.**
Even though beset with problems, my daughter does have a number of special talents and abilities. She is a superior reader and a natural star in her children's theater group. However, not every challenging child will be so blessed, and it would never be my intention to make a mother of a less fortunate child feel insecure in her quest for a healing. When I am in doubt of my boundaries, I bring to mind the fact that humble love does not call attention to personal success.

- **Love is never haughty or selfish or rude.**
Mothers of challenging children are not by nature either rude or haughty—our self-esteem has usually been beaten down too low. But there is the occasional problem of rudeness that comes with despair. I have caught myself in this rut a number of times. That's when I start feeling that

life has been unfair and everyone in my path is going to pay—especially slow or uninformed sales people, school officials, and well-meaning family members. This verse helps me remember that everything works better in an attitude of love. Gracious manners, no matter the situation, help keep me grounded in love, so that regardless of how I feel at the moment, I can release negative thoughts and move on with whatever needs to be done.

- **Love does not demand its own way.**
  When I first began to take my challenging child out with me into the world, I learned quickly that I wouldn't always get my own way. Sometimes the situation was between me and my child. I would have to give up on a desired behavior to accomplish another more important one. Sometimes it was with a teacher. Again, I would have to give up on one accommodation for my child in order to get proper help with an issue of more importance. Even today, whenever I'm frustrated, this passage reminds me to play every situation by ear and to be flexible. It also serves as a caution not to be self-serving—always bringing people into my problem—but to remain interested in their lives and needs.

- **Love is not irritable or touchy.**
  When everything is going wrong, I try to focus on this thought until I can exercise my bad mood away. I'm not always successful, but because of this verse I am at least aware of my goal and work on it.

- **Love does not hold grudges and will hardly even notice when others do it wrong.**
  When my child does wrong, I have to punish her, but this Scripture tells me not to hold on to my anger. There are

also times when her clever manipulation builds my feelings of resentment. The Bible reminds me that when I'm truly living in love, I'll hardly even notice her behavior.

- **Love is never glad about injustice, but rejoices whenever truth wins out.**
  I am never happy when my child has done wrong, but this verse points out that I should always be willing to pursue justice when she has been falsely accused. My challenging child needs to know that I honor truth above all else.

- **Love is loyal.**
  A loyal mother stands by her child in bad times as well as good. By now, I know this means gracefully accepting the disappointments and difficulties that come with a special needs child. It could also apply to my speaking well of her when there is no reason not to and to my always looking for the positive. (How easy it is to get into the habit of describing a child in negative tones.) This powerful Bible truth shows me that when I love with a loyal heart, I am building a relationship of trust.

  Though I would not want to oversimplify the concept of rearing a challenging child on love, it really does go back to the basic elementary truth learned in childhood Sunday school class. God is love. As his love touches our lives, we are granted the ability to love others with such compassion that no challenge is too great to confront. Love assures us of victory and celebration because whenever we are loving others, our mission is fulfilled and we have won our place on the road to successful parenting.

Dear Father, fill me with your wisdom so that I may rear your child now in my care. Give me the grace and strength necessary for the job. Grant me the zest and joy intended for the honor. Amen.

Confession

❧

My challenging child doesn't
measure up to his siblings.

TWENTY-ONE

❧

The Ugly Duckling—Again

LIKE IT OR NOT, THE DAY WILL COME when you look at your challenging child through a veil of sadness. You are feeling wistful about what might have been. I know because I have cried a few tears at this stage of life myself. I can even hear the secret conversations that never leave your heart. "At this age, Victoria was playing Chopin," or "Andy was quarterback and so popular with the other kids," or "Marisa was beautiful." In front of you stands a child who doesn't quite measure up. She is awkward and wears thick glasses. He is little and unmasculine. She is overweight and academically slow. He is untidy and smells bad. Perhaps he makes funny noises or jerks in unpleasant ways. Maybe people stare. Maybe they criticize or poke fun.

Meanwhile, your feelings surface in a pool of pity and renewed attempts to work harder on the child. Then follows the sense of shame because you know it is wrong to compare. You know it is wrong to wish for what isn't. You know it is wrong to want this child to be like another. And yet, even being equipped with the knowledge of your "wrongdoing," the thoughts and feelings are still there, so what could be *wrong* with you?

Nothing, aside from the fact that you are probably overly anxious. You are simply reacting the way all of us do after rearing a child or two before confronting our challenging one. By comparison, the others read like a book. We took them to dance class, and they danced. We stayed late for ball practice, and they became decent athletes. We dropped them off at school, and they learned. We may, in fact, have had very little to do with the success of these earlier children—a truth that leaves us feeling all the more nervous about the anemic performances of our challenging child. And all with good reason. For while the other children may have blossomed on their own, this is the one we will nurture to maturity.

But don't get discouraged or afraid. Though it may momentarily seem as if this child has been overlooked in the achievement department, we know it is simply not so. God gives all of his children equal amounts of goodness. Everything he has is for each one of us. And the great thing about these gifts is that they require no special ability, no hard-won lessons, and no particular style. A simple trust in Jesus Christ will do it all.

> But when the Holy Spirit controls our lives he will produce this kind of fruit in us: love, joy, peace, patience, kindness, goodness, faithfulness, gentleness and self-control.
>
> **Galatians 5:22-23a**

Wow! Could the mother of a challenging child ask for anything more? Isn't this what we've been wanting for our youngster all these years? Oh, I know it's not beauty or popularity or even recognizable talent, but take another look—these spiritually endowed qualities are the very things that make people movers and shakers. They are the actions that make a difference—the qualities that endure beyond age and the "right breaks." They are the qualities that can stand alone and be more than enough.

If your child has claimed Jesus as his Lord and Savior, these gifts of the Spirit belong to him now. However, you may have to help him discover his bounty. After all, this is a child who may not even know he can be kind and gentle and possess self-control. To me, his becoming aware of the fruit of the Spirit and then learning to utilize each gift is a part of the healing we as mothers pray for. Here are a few ways to help your child.

1. Begin by shaking off negative attitudes.

Adopt a "can do" approach in every area of your life. Strike negative and restrictive words such as *can't, shouldn't, ought, must,* etc. from your vocabulary. Strike out negative descriptions of your child such as *clumsy, poor reader, not mathematically inclined, couch potato, slow learner,* and so on. Replace these words and phrases with power-packed positive words. Try these words:

Instead of:	*Choose:*
should have	could have
need	want
can't	choose not to
have to	choose to
if	when

Encourage your child by using these phrases:
> You can do it.
> Go for it.
> You deserve the best you can give.
> Now is all there is.

Teach him to say:
> I can do it.
> I deserve the best I can give.

Remember this phrase for moments of camaraderie:
> I am always doing the best I can at the moment—and so are you.

2. Act as if your challenging child is already accomplished and well behaved.

Experts tell us that if we want to succeed in the business world we must dress and act as if we've already arrived. Do the same with your challenging child. Choose good teachers. See that he attends classes regularly. Take his hobbies and interests seriously, even though his attention span may tempt you to do otherwise. In short, act as if this child is the most talented and most cooperative youngster in the world.

3. Appreciate the differences in your challenging child.

God knew what he was doing when he created your son or daughter. Originality, persistence, and energy can be valuable assets when focused on following the path of truth. So relax, and let go of earlier expectations. When we release this child to God, we allow him to reach his highest potential, and no one is disappointed.

A Practical Idea Make a treasure map for your child. (See Appendix A.)

Dear God, enable me to see my child as you do—perfect and special in every way. Amen.

Confession

❧

I am ashamed that I think
more often of my child's
bad traits than her good ones.

TWENTY-TWO

❦

"Have You Seen My Child?"

SOON AFTER MY CHALLENGING CHILD WAS BORN, I purchased a lovely blank book with rabbits on the cover. I had kept a journal on my first child's infancy and knew enough about motherhood to realize I had best maintain the status quo by doing the same with my second one. This blank book would store the events of Alexandra's first year. But when her first birthday rolled around with only a few lines of rhyming verse in the book, it became apparent I would have to take a different approach. I did this by writing verse like this for every birthday.

Alexandra—My Five-Year-Old

Alexandra is mind over matter,
Will over mind,
A pop art painting,
A free form design.

Made in God's image
this child of mine grows,
The point of direction
Nobody knows.

I had no idea there was anything wrong with my child—only that she was "different" as well as stubborn and obstinate. So I tried my best to produce flattering themes for these poems that wouldn't come back to haunt me later. I wrote the most "telling" entry when my daughter was six years old. By this time, the task of writing something sweet and poetic about my child had become so difficult that I had to make a list of the things I liked about her to draw from. I never got any farther, and the list became that year's entry.

Things I Like About Xan:

1. She has big blue eyes.
2. She has soft, chubby hands that feel nice in mine.
3. She has a wonderful, raucous laugh.
4. She has an interesting college-student vocabulary.
5. She is bright and creative.
6. She is my child of six years.

I know challenging children abound with positive attributes, but their mothers are sometimes the last people to know about them. We are so busy dealing with the problems that we fail to notice the bonus or "flip" side of these youngsters. However, being aware of our children's strengths not only helps us provide the correct nurturing but can put new energy into our lives by reminding us we can enjoy, appreciate, and even be proud of our challenging child.

Because the term "challenging child" is used in this book to cover a wide range of behavior problems, it isn't possible to list specific strengths for you to look for in your child. But some of these positive characteristics are seen frequently enough throughout the gamut of behavior problems that you will no doubt nod your head in recognition at the mention of some of them.

Look for these traits in your child and smile.

- **Persistence.** A challenging child may be unusually persistent in getting his way. He won't let go of any denied or withheld request and will sometimes awake the next morning taking right up where he left off in his "badgering" spiel. Today you find this behavior a problem, but someday he could make a great salesman.

- **Friendliness.** A challenging child may be unusually friendly and outgoing. Sometimes this embarrasses you. It may even frighten you when you think about his willingness to talk and "go" with other people. Overall, there are few situations in the grown-up world where friendliness would not be considered an asset.

- **Energy.** A challenging child may be a high energy child. He may have sleep disorders and still be able to go at top speed throughout the day. This drives you crazy now, and probably makes him a fairly unwelcome guest at his grandparents'. But someday his work cohorts will envy this energy you now deplore.

- **Nerve.** A challenging child may know no fear. This has caused you a lot of anxiety—like the time he walked down the highway to go to a friend's house, or the time he stuck his finger in the light socket to "feel" electricity. You wonder if he'll make it to adulthood. But you can take comfort by knowing that if he does, his willingness to take risks without fearing them could make him a successful entrepreneur.

- **Uniqueness.** A challenging child may be "different" from other children in appearance and mannerisms. He frequently likes to wear hats and sometimes rearranges his clothes to produce offbeat color combinations. He may have an adultish vocabulary or be consumed with an unusual hobby.

Today you see this as a liability and spend time trying to make him appear more like his classmates. Being different is what could someday get him noticed in the art or entertainment world.

- **Exceptional talent.** A challenging child may have outstanding abilities in one skill he spends all of his time developing. You wish he'd work on a more balanced lifestyle. However, almost all star-quality performers have a one-track mind that helped them reach their goal.

- **Forthrightness.** A challenging child may be outspoken in his opinions. You've been embarrassed when he's asked your dinner guests why they're staying so late or told an adult he or she needs to go on a diet, but such honesty would be a welcome change in fields like career counseling or talent scouting where frankness combined with kindness could help direct people to their area of success.

These are only a few areas in which your challenging child may show unusual potential. Such examples show us we can almost always find a positive side to any annoying behavior or situation. Looking at what's right rather than thinking about what's wrong is more uplifting and emotionally rewarding than dwelling on the negative.

It was a kind and loving heavenly Father who had the forethought to endow each of our challenging children with unique personality traits. Often, these funny little quirks are the challenging child's ticket to a satisfactory relationship with other people, and we must be careful to cultivate the good that emerges from some of his negative habits. God hasn't quit writing the book on our children's lives and neither can we.

Fix your thoughts on what is true and good and right. Think about things that are pure and lovely, and dwell on the fine, good things in others.

Philippians 4:8b

A Practical Idea Fold a piece of paper in half. On one side, write down all the negative things your child does. On the other side, write down one good thing you could see as possibly resulting from the negative behaviors listed.

Dear God, you know I see the negative more readily than I see the positive. I ask you to open my eyes to all of the good you've placed in my child. Amen.

Confession

❧

I feel guilty when I have
to say no to my child.

TWENTY-THREE

"Have I Done Something Wrong?"

THERE HAVE BEEN MANY EVENINGS when my husband has poked his inquisitive face around the bedroom door during the fourth or fifth chapter of a bedtime story. Though he is careful not to interfere, I can tell by his facial expression that he wonders what's keeping me—how long can it take to tuck a child into bed? Later, I will explain, and my explanation will go something like this: "Well, you see, she wanted me to play a game with her earlier today, and I couldn't. I just felt so guilty that I wanted to make it up to her."

Or perhaps I let my daughter stay up an extra hour because when she asked me to read to her earlier in the evening I was engrossed in my own pleasure reading and said no.

Guilt has been a masterful enemy in the parenting of this child, for the challenging child craves attention and self-gratification to the point of addiction and can be very resourceful in getting his way. A dictionary definition says guilt is the fact of being responsible for an offense or wrongdoing—remorseful awareness of having done something wrong.

As Christians we know we don't have to carry around our guilt. We know our guilt can be absolved. When we confess our sins to Jesus, we begin life anew with a clean slate.

Now God says he will accept and acquit us—declare us "not guilty"—if we trust Jesus Christ to take away our sins.

Romans 3:21b

This is not the type of guilt that threatens my peace of mind. No, my guilt, and I suspect that of many women, stems from the preconceived idea that my role as mother to my challenging child involves the responsibility of providing a conflict-free environment. Perhaps you'll recognize some of these common, guilt-controlled situations:

- *A mother buys her child a toy because she feels badly about disciplining earlier in the day.*

- *A mother gives in to her child's request for candy because she's about to leave home for a meeting.*

- *A mother allows her child to stay up late because she was especially strict about the child eating his dinner.*

These and other guilt-powered actions have a way of multiplying until one day we realize we have confused love with approval. We have given our child everything he wanted, but in so doing, we have denied him a parent.

If you are in such a predicament, decide today to step out of this destructive role. We are, in fact, often surprised at how easy it is to change this habit when we stop to think a few things through. First, we have to recognize that our children need our guidance. While it sounds like great fun to be our child's best friend, we have certain responsibilities that outweigh our child's approval. We have to help our children with their problems, minister to their physical needs, and teach them our values. Some of these lessons will involve conflict and our having to say no.

Here are a few common situations that cause guilt along with an explanation of how mothers *should* feel when confronted with a similar incident.

- **Sometimes when we say no to our child's request for time, we feel guilty because, in truth, we really didn't want to spend time with him.** We need to understand that when we say no in this situation, we're really just wanting some time to ourselves. Mothers of challenging children need time to refresh and renew their spirits on a regular basis.

- **When we refuse to buy our child an item at the store, we feel guilty because we have something in the shopping basket for ourselves.** Remember, overindulgence is not an honest preparation for life. When we overindulge our children, we are not doing them any good. Life doesn't indulge us, and we should try to prepare our youngsters for what life is really like. Children don't have to have something just because they are with us when we are shopping for ourselves. Besides, sometimes we shop just for them.

- **We feel guilty when we say no to buying a toy out of the prin-ciple that our child has too many toys.** Keep in mind that, over the long haul, buying things doesn't take the place of *doing* things. Buying something will never compensate for not playing ball, not reading a story, not going on a nature walk, and all the hundreds of other little things we as parents would sometimes rather not do.

Parenting isn't a popularity contest. There are many times when, just because we're the accountable ones, we have to create protective boundaries. Bedtimes, eating habits, and social privileges are just some of the areas in which parents have to lead. If you think being a pushover does your child a favor, what do you think it teaches about stability and strength of character?

Not to make any of this sound too easy; challenging children are especially able to manipulate mom's emotions. Often, it's their intensely unhappy struggle with life that causes us to want to make up for everything that's not right. One way to override our children's persistence and guilt-provoking action is to stay within the moment. When we're concentrating on this very moment, there is no need to use the past as our reference on how to act now. We do what is right for now with a show of confidence.

I am always amazed at such times to discover that once the hysterics are over, my child is relatively pleasant, giving no indication she thinks I should feel guilty. This shows that many of the things we don't want to give or do for our children are not really so "wanted" anyway.

> Don't copy the behavior and customs of this world, but be a new and different person with a fresh newness in all you do and think. Then you will learn from your own experience how his ways will really satisfy you.
>
> **Romans 12:2**

A Practical Idea Making a list of what you will and will not do, or allow others to do, will help you focus on the moment. When your child makes a request to which you must say no, find it on the list, and read the statement to him. He may still go on and on with his pleas, but you will find it easier to stay in control and avoid guilt feelings if you have a ready-made guideline. Your list might be a simple rundown of house rules such as:

- There will be no television before leaving for school.

- Snacks must be eaten by 9:00 P.M.

- You may not play with a friend until you've completed all homework.

Your list could also serve to enforce the training of new skills. For example, in the back of one of my old notebooks, under the title "Alexandra," is this sentence: "Mother will not be combing anyone's hair this week." I wrote this during a period when I was encouraging my daughter (against her will) to take responsibility for her personal grooming. Whenever she came to me with her hair brush, I turned to this page in my notebook, and she knew instantly that she was not going to talk me into doing her job.

Of course, it is impossible to think of every situation ahead of time. For those times, remember that when we give in to guilt, we have relinquished not only our power but our guidance and leadership.

Dear Father, give me the strength to say no and the grace to feel good about it so my child will grow more like you. Amen.

Confession

꧁꧂

I am always lonely. There are no other
moms out there in my situation.

TWENTY-FOUR

Home Alone

NOTHING VALIDATES OUR PRESENCE ON EARTH like the companionship of a good friend. But it's not unusual for the mother of a challenging child to feel cut off from the rest of the world. The worst of it is, it's not just a feeling. Our perception of isolation is as real as the limits it sets for us.

True, some of our isolation is self-inflicted, but not because we want it that way.

Problems tend to make people go inward, and the problem of a hard-to-manage child is often viewed as a private shame. Hostility, disapproval, and patronizing pity are just some of the reactions we may encounter from others. No wonder we think it's easier not to explain our child's unusual behavior—easier not to make special arrangements—easier to just stop trying.

At other times, our loneliness is the result of social stigma. Mothers of challenging children don't always fit into the "group." Our needs are not always the same as those of other mothers. Our child doesn't play well with the other children. Sometimes even our idea of a good time is different from that of other mothers. Though disappointing, it's understandable when our phone stops ringing and our name is dropped from invitation lists. In all honesty, we are social liabilities.

What we really need is a friend tailor-made just for us, but in reality, we're not particular. Anyone with the ability to create a feeling of intimacy could begin the healing of our hearts.

Unfortunately, friendships are not easily cemented during the child-rearing years. In today's mobile, fast-paced society, it often seems that everyone is too busy, too tired, or too "distant" for committed relationships outside of the family. Other people's disinterest in forming friendships can feel especially distressing if we have been seeking out of need. Perhaps we have sincerely followed the age-old adage that "to have a friend, one must first be a friend," and our efforts have still gone unrewarded. If so, now is the time to carry the statement one step further. Try being a friend to yourself.

You see, I happen to know from personal experience that mothers of challenging children don't often like the person dominating their psyche. When we look in the mirror, we see an unlikable person.

- She is depressed.
- Her child is a failure.
- She is fat.
- She is bone thin.
- She is lazy.
- She is cranky.
- She is unlovable.
- Most of all, she is not anybody we would want as a friend.

I am not going to tell you it's time to change—to become more suitable, try a little harder, adapt, and readjust. I'm just going to suggest that you take another look at that person in the mirror. Actually, this is no ordinary human being staring back at you. This person is extraordinary. This person is walking the earth with purpose. She is beautiful, intelligent, and interesting. She is certain of her reason for being, and her life confidently expresses fulfillment. Certainly, she is likable and a pleasure to be around. But she is not in particular need of a friend. God has already given her the best friend she will ever have—himself.

Though you may not believe it right now, this person in the mirror is you. Your purpose is your child. As you give to him or her, the world gives back to you, and you are indeed the beautiful, intelligent, interesting woman of your dreams. Your empty hours are filled with meaningful activities that enhance the lives of others. And as you move gracefully through life with divine direction, loneliness becomes a thing of the past.

Yet I will not be alone, for the Father is with me.

John 16:32b

A Practical Idea God will always be there in some way that we can recognize and understand. Look for his presence in everyday activities. He may make himself known through the attention of a caring neighbor. (Seniors are some of the best allies a lonely mom can have. Though most do not like to baby-sit, they do like younger women and have a great deal to offer in a friendship. They are also very nice about tolerating your child as long as you are there beside him.)

Another way God's presence can comfort us is through a good television show. Informative, upbeat shows can bring a sense of well-being into our home and lift our spirits. Make an appointment with yourself for one hour of constructive television viewing.

Sometimes a really good book can stimulate us with God-given energy and enthusiasm for life. For the duration of the book and perhaps a short time afterwards, we are friends with the author and the characters in the book. If you become a regular at the library, you'll find yourself forming a loose friendship with the library staff. All of these superficial contacts are important when we're feeling friendless.

Remain active in any women's organization you may have considered giving up because of the demands of your challenging child. Even when your situation causes you to feel apart from others, time spent away from your child and in the company of other women can momentarily take the edge off of loneliness.

And of course, there is always the healing power of meditation and prayer. A lonely woman should make a huge effort to reserve herself a quiet time because, when we take our loneliness to God, he restores us and sustains us with a sense of peace.

Perhaps one of the best ways to find new friends through the presence of God is to follow where he leads. Whenever we feel a calling to perform a particular act of kindness, it's important to follow through. For one thing, it's impossible to be lonely when we're helping others. For another, we know that God's paths always lead to our highest good. This is why he really is all that we need.

Dear Father, thank you for being my friend. I love you. Amen.

Confession

~~≈~~

I am so tired;
I feel that I shortchange my
other child on a daily basis.

TWENTY-FIVE

Forgotten Family

I WAS SURPRISED TO LEARN THAT MY OLDEST DAUGHTER, away at college, was homesick.

"Why on earth are you surprised?" my mother asked. "Heather always was a homebody."

"Of course," I answered nonchalantly.

But as I spoke, a bolt of reality struck my comfort zone.

The problem was, I didn't really know this "good" child as well as I would like. Always obedient, always compliant, always good-natured and helpful—this was the child to slip through my fingers in the midst of our family's struggle with her challenging sibling.

Such things happen to a family in crisis, even a loving and caring family. Certainly, no well-meaning parent would purposely overlook one child in favor of another, but it happens on the sly—slowly, steadily, unrelentingly because the challenging child never lets up in his battle for dominance.

He is the one you know through and through because he is your attention seeker. He wants your undivided attention every moment of the day. And you are well aware that he gets it. In a million different ways, pulling from his catalog of creativity, his charismatic personality, or maybe even his temper.

Ironically, it doesn't matter whether the attention is favorable or not. He simply wants you to focus on him. Soon, every facet of family life is in his command—holidays, special occasions, even ordinary week nights are shattered by this one child's constant demands or disruptive behavior. There are no "good" times for just talking or chumming around with other family members. You are being totally consumed by your challenging child's needs. While he drains energy from you like a vacuum hose, the rest of your family learns to fend for themselves. They are your "forgotten children," for even though you have not forgotten them in the literal sense, they sometimes feel as though you have.

Perhaps your "forgotten ones" have simply given up on the issue. You see this in their resignation of personal rights. At some point, the bully's actions have become unchallenged. They are accepted norms at home, and family members quickly learn that it is easier to give in than to hold out. You say nothing because, after all, peace is your most precious commodity. Your older children, on the other hand, may react with avoidance. As long as they stay busy and away from home as much as possible, they can pretend the problem doesn't exist. Once home, however, it is next to impossible not to hear these older siblings' complaints and criticisms.

"Why don't you ever make him behave?"

"You never let me get away with things like that."

"Mom, I'm not taking him—he embarrasses me."

"Can't you do something with her?"

"What about the way I feel?"

(Of course, there is also the possibility the older or brighter siblings contribute to family discord by antagonizing the challenging child into disruptive behavior, but that is another matter.)

What does a mother do when one child tugs more strongly than the others? Should she be concerned about fairness? Should she make the other children simply share the burden? Should she set limits on what she gives to one child so that there is enough of her to go around? If questions like these crowd your thinking, be aware that God supports you in the care and nurturing of your entire family—not just your challenging child.

A family is the most loving, caring association we can ever have on earth. No other group of people will ever accept us as unconditionally as those within our family unit. No one else will understand us as well or so readily forgive our shortcomings. Even today, in busy, sophisticated times, the family is one of God's greatest gifts.

Surely, one of our roles as women and mothers is to honor our family's association and protect it from disintegration. But this is a goal that is easier said than done. In fact, with most forces in today's world working openly against the family, there may be only one way to truly succeed at such action, and that is to totally dedicate ourselves to the pursuit of harmonious family life. Though it sounds corny on the surface, success in any area is never won without hard work. A healthy, happy, functional family is no exception.

Unfortunately, too many of us are unwilling to put forth the effort to get a rich, fulfilling family life. We want to believe it is out of our control—that the distress within our homes is something that has simply happened to us, certainly not something we've allowed to occur. We need to realize that life is not as out of control as it may seem. I believe life flows naturally toward harmony, and our attitude either contributes to its progress or inhibits its growth.

Does your family seem disconnected or lacking in harmony? If so, perhaps it's time to consider the following dedication proposal.

I (*your name*) dedicate my life to establishing family harmony so that all members will feel valued and loved.

1. I will dedicate my voice to harmony.

Do you respond to anger by raising your voice? (Most of us do.) And yet, most of us will also agree that our challenging child, at whom the anger is most often directed, doesn't even seem to hear us. Meanwhile, our harsh, strident tones have a way of intimidating the more sensitive family members. If this is a problem with you, find another way to express anger. I've found that my challenging child responds better to a written note of reprimand than to a verbal complaint. If your child doesn't read, however, you may want to try saving your lowest voice for moments of serious reprimands.

You'll also find that harmony is enhanced when everyday talk is primarily positive rather than negative. Other children in the family can feel emotionally "pulled down" by mom's constant complaints about the challenging child.

Gentle words cause life and health; griping brings discouragement. **Proverbs 15:4**

2. I will dedicate my judgment to harmony.

Do your "forgotten children" keep messy rooms and perform chores sloppily? Are they underachievers who could perform better at school if they would? Though it is important to teach children to do things properly, give special consideration in all areas during times of crisis—and living with a challenging sibling is definitely a crisis. Go easy on these kids. Remember that, like you, they are under stress. Empathize with them rather than get angry.

3. I will dedicate my sense of awareness to harmony.

Though we willingly provide material needs for all of our children, our "forgotten children" sometimes fall short of our attention. It's important for mothers to notice and appreciate the unique contribution each child makes to the family. But in order to do so, we have to become aware of each child's needs and stay sensitive to each child's feelings. Once we have acknowledged that it's not any easier to have a challenging sibling than it is to be a mother to a challenging child, we are more likely to nurture all of our children with the same amount of energy.

Here are ways to nurture with awareness:

- **Give the gift of encouragement.** Smile. Say a good word. Hug. Verbally acknowledge that you are proud of this child's behavior, scholastic record, and so on.

- **Give the gift of an attentive ear.** You have one child who never stops talking. Sensing your need for quiet, your "forgotten children" may purposely hold back. Don't assume they have nothing to share. Invite their conversation. These children have concerns and joys that need a parent's attention and affirmations.

- **Give the gift of prayer.** While you hold your challenging child up to the Lord, don't overlook your "forgotten children." All of our children need and deserve God's blessings.

- **Give the gift of recognition.** Support your "forgotten children's" extracurricular activities with your praise and attendance. Often, it's the little things that count. For example, when I realized my lack of enthusiasm belittled my older child's drill team activity, I decided to affirm her by celebrating each game morning with a small gift at the breakfast table. I purchased all of the tokens at one time and marked my calendar to remember the game dates. I was ashamed when my daughter showed such surprise at being singled out as special. It made me realize how negligent I had been.

Of course, there are many innovative ways to demonstrate our love. Share a good book. Cook a favorite dish. Watch a special television show together. A college-age child will appreciate a mailbox full of letters from home. Don't forget the value of your presence. All ages will enjoy one-on-one time with mom—perhaps Saturday lunch at a restaurant or an evening trip to the mall. And yes, your challenging child will make these occasions very difficult to carry off, but you must go ahead in spite of the difficulties because your "forgotten child" needs you, too.

Jesus loves all children. For him, there is no such thing as a "forgotten child." He loves each one with a love that is great enough to go around, even in a family with a challenging child. This is why none of us should even try to handle the job of mothering by ourselves. We need a partner who is all-knowing. We need an ally who is all-conquering. We need an assistant who can stretch our patience and perseverance. So, what else is new? The answer. The answer to our superhuman needs is the superhuman power of God. By ourselves, living with a challenging child can be pure hell for everyone in the family. But we can transcend the human limitations that cause disharmony. When we agree to work with God, we become a channel for divine love, and everything once so impossible is now possible. We help create peace and a feeling of belonging for each member of the family. No one is forgotten. Each child is secure in our bountiful love and attention. At last our home life reveals our love for each other and becomes a testimony of our oneness with God.

See my servant, whom I uphold; my Chosen One, in whom I delight. I have put my Spirit upon him; he will reveal justice to the nations of the world. He will be gentle—he will not shout nor quarrel in the streets. He will not break the bruised reed, nor quench the dimly burning flame. He will encourage the fainthearted, those tempted to despair. He will see full justice given to all who have been wronged. He won't be satisfied until truth and righteousness prevail throughout the earth, nor until even distant lands beyond the seas have put their trust in him.

Isaiah 42:1-4

A Practical Idea In the appendix of this book, you will find some special activities to do with or for your challenging child. Complete one of these projects for each of your other children, too. Don't ask. Often, your other children will sense your fatigue and claim disinterest. Nor should you anticipate kudos. Sometimes we don't know for years how important a particular action of love meant at the time. Just rest assured that regardless of the *reaction*, your efforts will be cherished somewhere down the line.

Dear God, thank you for holding each one of us dear in the family of God. Help me to nurture and love each of my children in a special way. Amen.

Confession

~~☙~~

I feel sorry for myself.
I resent the fact that my life must be
spent on this impossible child.

TWENTY-SIX

Accepting the Gift

Do you ever wonder why your life was chosen to be complicated by the presence of a challenging child?

I do.

Sometimes when all semblance of sanity has left my household, I look enviously at those families composed of only "normal" children and begin to question the fairness of life. *God did something unkind to me,* I think to myself. *Other mothers have it easier and better than I.* Or, *Maybe I'm being punished for something—did I really do anything that bad?*

Usually by the time the particular crisis that initiated such feelings has passed, I'm more levelheaded. By this time, I realize it could be worse. I could be paralyzed and have to deal with my child from the bed. I could have had quintuplets—all of them challenging. I could have a terminal illness and not get to finish my mothering job.

All of these thoughts hold my self-pity somewhat in check so that I'm soon able to get back to work. Only rarely, however, do I feel centered enough to recognize the truth: This problem, which looms above me like a dark cloud, is perhaps the single biggest opportunity of my life.

Opportunity? A challenging child? A child whose demands keep me constantly on the go without a moment of peace?

Yes. And here is why. A challenging child presents a problem. Though problems are inconvenient and troublesome, to say the least, there is something good to be gained from them as well. Problems help us grow. We grow when we relinquish our need to be in control and begin depending upon God for the solution. We grow when we set a goal. We grow when we seek help and information.

When we have a problem, we will grow in every way God intends for us to grow.

"But for the duration of raising a child?" you ask, "How can I deal with a problem that is so drawn out?"

By working on it in small ways, day by day. By thinking on the lessons to be learned rather than the time involved. By being grateful for the problem itself.

Grateful?

Yes. Because the presence of our problem is proof that God is not through with us. He sees within us room for improvement and great potential. God knows that each one of us can attain wisdom and maturity through hard work. So this problem that has become the bane of our existence is actually our pathway to growth.

It is also our call to service. Maybe we can't see any connection between getting through the day with a challenging child and serving the Lord because it's not our idea of service. And yet there's no denying this is where we are. God placed us here to accept a mission of "unknown" importance. Though we may not see the scope of our influence for years to come, we can be sure of its purpose and impact on the glory of his kingdom.

God in heaven appoints each man's work.

John 3:27

Once we are able to see our role in God's plan, the situation we've labeled a problem becomes a gift. Accept it with humility, love, humor, and enjoyment, and God will lead you to the solution eventually. There is no merit in trying to outsmart the problem of a challenging child by resisting or rushing through his childhood; there is no fast or easy out. We will have this problem until we learn the lesson. But never forget that we are not on this journey alone. God is with us. Furthermore, he will never give us a problem greater than our inner strength.

Is your life full of difficulties and temptations? Then be happy, for when the way is rough, your patience has a chance to grow. So let it grow, and don't try to squirm out of your problems. For when your patience is finally in full bloom, then you will be ready for anything, strong in character, full and complete.

James 1:2-4

A Practical Idea If your challenging child is your mission, then you have become a missionary. Congratulations! A mission is a wonderful blessing. If you don't believe it, take a closer look at career missionaries. You'll notice that some glow with enthusiasm for their work. When they talk about sacrifices and hardships, it can sound like a Disney World ride rather than an inconvenience. When they encounter illness or hostility, it is nothing but a mere annoyance. When they are in the States, they want to be back on the field. When they are on the field, they never wish to be back in the States. What's more, you'll often find the children of these missionaries as excited about missions as their parents. If it all sounds a little unbelievable to you, I can understand, but there is nothing really unusual going on here, it is simply the fulfillment of God's Word.

Before Jesus ascended to heaven, he challenged all believers to spread his love throughout the world and promised that those who did would have every power necessary to complete the job.

You are to go into all the world and preach the Good News to everyone, everywhere. Those who believe and are baptized will be saved. But those who refuse to believe will be condemned. And those who believe shall use my authority to cast out demons, and they shall speak new languages. They will be able even to handle snakes with safety, and if they drink anything poisonous, it won't hurt them; and they will be able to place their hands on the sick and heal them.

Mark 16:15-18

So your child is not "everyone" and your home not "everywhere." It doesn't matter. Jesus wants each soul to enter his kingdom, and every home to shine with his light. Perhaps worldly invasions of modern-day evils make the home the most exotic mission field of all. At any rate, once you've answered the call to missions, you can immediately begin discovering the blessings of missionary life. Here are a few guidelines:

- **Begin each day by inviting God to do something wonderful through you.**

- **Take your job seriously.** Give thought to what you hope to accomplish for your child in the year ahead, and consider what you can actually do to help bring it about. Look at various aspects of his life, such as educational, social, and spiritual, and make a plan that will assist him in each area. Keep records to track your progress.

- **Act with enthusiasm.** Speak in an excited tone when talking to others about your life. Let them know that you love it—great things are happening, and you are so happy to be involved in such a great mission.

- **Act with confidence.** Not only when others question your decisions regarding issues such as education, but at home when you begin to doubt your parenting abilities. Always remember, you have been well equipped to complete your mission. Jesus understood the power of the world and has made you stronger.

But what if you secretly believe that God has made a terrible mistake? What if this child who stands before you is not the type of person you had in mind when saying yes to the call of motherhood? Maybe you imagined a beautiful child with perfect behavior and astounding intelligence. A child who was so easy to care for that you went right on with your satisfying career. Maybe you dreamed of a child who, through your knowledgeable guidance, would show the world "how Christian children act": what good friends they make, what excellent students they are, what model citizens they become.

Like the missionary called to serve in Italy but assigned by his board to work in West Africa, you were naturally disappointed and felt quite unprepared when given your challenging child. Today, the situation you face is not the perfect scenario you once imagined, and just as a misplaced missionary often asks for a transfer, you have been "putting in for a change" by mentally concentrating on what is not. This is the point at which it's important to remember that while it may not be what you expected, whatever is going on in your life today is part of God's plan.

It has been my personal experience that God never just compensates for a change of plans—he always overcompensates. You can spend a lifetime reflecting on past events—wishing for what isn't, dreaming about what could be. In so doing, you'll miss the joy of what is. Helping your child reach his potential will never be one of the glamour careers, but such an assignment does have its moments of satisfaction and joy that only come freely when we give ourselves to the ministry of serving God in whatever way in whatever part of the world he wants. Isn't this really what Jesus meant by going into the world and preaching the good news to everyone—everywhere?

Father God, help me to accept my mission in life with thankfulness and a willingness to give it my best. Amen.

Confession

❧

When my child says, "I'm sorry,"
I don't always want to
forgive and forget.

TWENTY-SEVEN

❧

Apologies Accepted

THE BAD-MOOD CHILD CAN TEST A MOTHER'S RESOLVE at every turn. Here is a child who swings from high spirits to low at the drop of a hat. Call it impulsiveness, aggressiveness, poor anger control, or resistance—inappropriate behavior is still inappropriate behavior. While most of us can handle a certain amount of inappropriate antics, there is always the one big wave of anger that carries us where we're no longer ourselves.

Chances are your challenging child doesn't want to be a problem. Studies indicate that mood is directly linked to brain patterns—something which is out of his control. Yet you may know that he is uncomfortable with his misbehavior because "mistakes" are often followed by quick apologies. On the surface, this looks fairly promising. If you are like me, however, the problem is that sometimes his pleas for forgiveness hit you the wrong way. Perhaps you know that as soon as you've said, "Yes, I forgive you," the act will be repeated. Or maybe your moods take longer to build than his do. You who are normally a pillar of patience and forbearance, once broken, may now want to nurse your hurt a little longer. My advice is: don't. Your anger will only serve to accelerate anxiety in your child—a reaction that could ultimately result in even greater discord between the two of you. Besides, there is a key to forgiveness that will change your outlook on apologies and enable you to get on with the business of mothering with amazing ease. It's called letting go.

So often we think of forgiveness as condoning the action—a way of saying that whatever was done is, in fact, all right. How can we approve of our child talking back to us, breaking important rules, or trying to hurt us physically? The very idea makes us angry all over again. That's what makes the act of letting go so much easier. When we let go of an incident, we no longer have to approve or disapprove of the action. We are completely freed from the scene.

Anger, guilt, jealousy, the need to control go out the window in the process of letting go. We no longer act on the incident or feeling. We don't talk about it. We don't daydream about it. We don't keep a mental scoreboard. The incident no longer exists. We have let it go to make room for a higher, better thought.

How much do we let go? All the way. Every single little quibble must be put aside and out of mind in order to make room for our good.

How often do we let go? Over and over.

Then Peter came to him (Jesus) and asked, "Sir, how often should I forgive a brother who sins against me? Seven times?"

"No!" Jesus replied, "seventy times seven!"

Matthew 18:21-22

Jesus meant that we shouldn't keep a record of how many times we forgive someone because there is no limit to the number of times we can forgive and start over.

Don't, however, assume that letting go should come easily and, if it doesn't, that something is wrong with you. Jesus wrestled with his demons for forty days (see Matthew 4:1-11). It may take days or months to truly let go for the first time. Then, too, there is such a thing as meeting the granddaddy of all beasts—coming face to face with the one thing we can't seem to let go of.

When this happens, remember that forgiveness is freedom to move on. Spend time each day focusing on truth by reading your Bible. Treat yourself to support and tolerance through carefully chosen friends and contacts. If you still can't bring yourself to look at your child and say, "I forgive you," let the Holy Spirit help you out. Tell your child that yes, through the enabling love of Christ, you forgive him. Repeat this phrase to yourself throughout the day whenever the bad feeling tries to surface. You will be surprised how soon you have truly forgiven.

An Affirmation for Letting Go

Through Jesus Christ, I forgive you.
I release my anger and let it go.
I am free—you are free.
Peace and happiness connect us
and all is well.

One of the nicest things about letting go is that it enables us to look at the situation through different eyes. For instance, when dealing with our challenging child, it's important to look beyond his shortcomings to the qualities that are yet to be. You know he is a work in progress. Within that child who has pushed you beyond all reasonable limits is an expression of our Father God, maker of heaven and earth. God's love will triumph, regardless. But your forgiveness of the child gives him a more comfortable space for his continued growth and frees you to walk the rest of your journey with renewed physical, emotional, and spiritual power.

Whatever you bind on earth is bound in heaven, and whatever you free on earth will be freed in heaven.

Matthew 18:18

A Practical Idea Letting go of grudges and past hurts does not mean we do not discipline a challenging child. This is a child who by his very nature requires firm, consistent discipline. Forgiveness, however, is an act that should happen simultaneously with the discipline. You will frequently hear your challenging child challenge your discipline with this kind of statement: "But you said you forgave me! Why are you still punishing me?" This is when you must reply lovingly but firmly, "Yes, I do forgive you, but I still have to punish you because I am training you not to do this again."

Punishment and forgiveness can be very confusing for both parents and children. It's not so difficult if the punishment comes first and then the child asks for forgiveness. But it is always hard when the child asks for forgiveness before the punishment has been doled out. Perhaps the single most important thing to remember is that you must pay attention and discipline before you become so angry that the matter of forgiveness is an issue. You'll discover that when you step in early enough, your discipline has nothing to do with anger but is solely a tool for training.

Finally, if you are still having trouble with forgiveness, perhaps there is something in your life for which you haven't forgiven yourself. Often the remembrance of past sin still brings a "sting" even after we've asked God for forgiveness. Remember, when we confess our sins to Jesus Christ, our sins are forgiven, and we no longer need to punish ourselves by feeling the pain.

Dear God, help me to forgive my child, just as you have already forgiven me. Amen.

Confession

❧

Sometimes I think I'm crazy to pray
that God will heal my child.

TWENTY-EIGHT

Coping and Hoping

THERE IS A SAYING AMONG PARENTS of challenging children that goes something like this: "Stop looking for a cure and start learning how to cope."

Those words can seem terribly brutal to a mother who wants and needs to hang on to hope. Hearing them for the first time is kind of like receiving a poor prognosis: "There's nothing else that can be done for your child, so get over it and deal with it."

I don't think anyone ever intended the statement to be anything but helpful. It is primarily a statement meant to motivate and encourage. However, I admit that hearing it once gave me reason to ponder my own choice of a healing journey. I began to wonder if a "cure" was the same as a "healing." If so, perhaps I was wasting my time believing that ultimate good would one day come out of my child's confused and disruptive nature.

So, for a period of time, I was pessimistic and unhappy. I didn't think I could continue without the hope that one day my child's troubling behavior would be replaced with a life of peace and happiness. Then slowly I began to hear the truth behind the words. The truth I heard was that God begins to answer our prayer for healing the moment we ask. And just because we may not see physical evidence of improvement doesn't mean that the answer is no. We don't always know what the answer is. But we do know that when God has begun a good work within us, he will not stop until the work is finished. Our God is a God of healing.

But he is also a God of practical matters.

Mark out a straight, smooth path for your feet so that those who follow you, though weak and lame, will not fall and hurt themselves, but become strong.

Hebrews 12:13

Coping is perhaps the practical aspect of divine healing. Through coping, we clear a path for hope, which is necessary for building an optimistic outlook for our child's future. What we hope is to see this child develop into a calm spirit who lives with an attitude of love, knows joy and peace, and reacts to life's daily events with patience and kindness. We hope he will grow into the kind of individual who will be good to others and faithful to his beliefs. But most of all, we fervently hope he can one day practice self-control. Hope underscores the unlimited possibilities our child possesses regardless of his particular problem. Hope gives us the strength to manage and the power to wait.

But if we must keep trusting God for something that hasn't happened yet, it teaches us to wait patiently and confidently.

Romans 8:25

And this is where the coping comes in. Because healing knows no time frame, we must find some way to get through the period of waiting. It could be a lifetime before we see improvement—if improvement is, in fact, to be a part of God's plan. Meanwhile, we have a family to rear, a marriage to hold together, sometimes an outside job to complete. Learning how to cope with things as they are is imperative.

Since my daughter's diagnosis, there have been remarkable advances in public awareness and understanding of some of the more common behavior disorders and the creation of a number of aids to help families cope with this problem. Several national organizations offer information and camaraderie. Television, newspapers, and magazines have featured some of the disorders in a positive, informational format. Public libraries across the country have made an earnest attempt to keep as much up-to-date material on the subject as possible on their shelves. Educational rights have been studied and adjusted to meet the needs of the learning disabilities children with behavior disorders often have. All this is in addition to the immense boost the medical community's innovative use of medications has given some families.

It's nice to know that today, the parents of newly diagnosed children can start out more informed and better equipped to cope with their situation than my husband and I were. But if you are this minute feeling that your own child's situation is different because you are certain of its hopelessness—certain beyond a doubt that no miraculous coping action could ever make things better—take a few deep breaths and give your thoughts the freedom to move to a higher place. There is such a thing as learning to cope spiritually. While the benefits of such coping are intangible, taking the steps to reach this type of peace and happiness will greatly benefit you throughout your life in other areas as well.

- **Learn to cope by reading the Bible.**
  Use a concordance and look up every verse you can find under the heading "healing." You will be amazed at the number and variety of "true life stories" included in the Scriptures on this subject. These stories are not there for historical or sociological purposes. They are there to illustrate God's power and compassion. They are there to feed

us with belief and hope. And they are there to show us that we, too, can bring loved ones to the healing presence of God through prayer.

A few suggestions to get you started:

Read about Elisha restoring a child to life (see 2 Kings 4:8-37).

Read about Jesus sending a demon out of a woman's daughter (see Matthew 15:21-28).

Read about Jesus healing a man's son (see John 4:46-54).

So, you think you have a hopeless case? That's all right. Each one of these stories is about as hopeless as you can get. But God healed them anyway.

- **Learn to cope by living in the present.**
  When you position yourself in the present, you will soon see that hope is not for tomorrow or the day after, it's for now—this moment in which you feel so helpless. Hope is for strengthening your stance. When things seem like they can only get worse, hope is your promise that it will one day get better.

  You will have courage because you will have hope.
  You will take your time, and rest in safety.

  Job 11:18

- **Learn to cope by making a list of affirmations.**
  Create a list of positive statements and encouraging quotes or Bible verses. Put them on your bathroom mirror, print them on notecards to slip into your purse, and commit them to memory for moments of weakness. We take a step toward God when we voice our hope. It is a way of turning our attention from the difficulty to praising God for whatever solution he offers. It works.

You can get anything—anything you ask for in prayer—if you believe.

Matthew 21:22

And so, Lord, my only hope is in you.

Psalms 39:7

I will keep on expecting you to help me.

Psalms 71:14a

- **Learn to cope by creating a *Book of Hope*.**
  This is a collection of newspaper articles covering good news stories about people who have succeeded in spite of various physical or social handicaps. It can be similar to an image book in which one cuts pictures and words out of magazines that describe the person he wants to be. You can elaborate on this concept by including a portion in your book that describes the person you know your child to be. You may even want to make a section for the person you are striving to become, highlighting those qualities you want to develop on this arduous journey.

- **Learn to cope by getting help from professionals who are not likely to criticize your spiritual stance and who are always willing to keep trying new ideas.**
  When your child's physician or therapist says, "This is all we can do," you know that you have reached a kind of road block and that you must now choose another route. It's fine to obtain recommendations from other parents of challenging children, but do so with the realization that a successful doctor-patient relationship has a great deal to do with chemistry. What suits your friend may not help you at all. Don't be ashamed to keep searching.

Sometimes, in spite of our faithful pursuit of coping abilities, we are unable to see hope in the future or feel peace in the present. With such a bleak outlook, there seems little reason to keep trying so hard.

Diminished hope is often caused by lack of progress. At least for the time being, your child shows no improvement and you suffer. Need I remind you that the journey has not yet ended? If there is a lack of progress, it is because you and your child are simply in a holding pattern like airplanes that must circle a city before landing. Just as there is a reason for a delayed aircraft landing, so there is a reason for your having to wait. Waiting offers an excellent opportunity for learning. And if you have not mastered patience and acceptance, the lessons are still yours to learn.

In the meantime, give yourself LOVE. Here is an acronym of unknown source that will help you attend your own needs while taking care of your child's.

L — You must learn your limitations.
O — You must remember that you are only one person and can't possibly do it all.
V — You must visualize a brighter future.
E — You must receive encouragement from others.

Rely on positive people for hope-filled moments. Tell them you need a word of encouragement. Tell them what to say if necessary. Sometimes we know the truth but need to hear it from another person's mouth.

God doesn't give us hopeless cases. Your son or daughter is one of his wonderful children—a spiritual being with every hope for a life of successful living. Perhaps he will stay in a holding pattern indefinitely. But this, too, is okay when we understand that sometimes coping means relying upon God to restore peace in our thinking and give us the hope that enables us to see beyond our present situation to a future of possibilities.

A Practical Idea The passages of human growth are typically burdened with a variety of transitions, each stressful enough to test the most advanced life-coping skills. Career disappointments or failure, death and bereavement, middle age, the empty nest, retirement, violence, terrorism, and war are just some of the possible life events we may be asked to confront and cope with some day. Of course, this doesn't mean our present situation isn't stressful, but it does suggest that perhaps now is the *best* time to master those all-important methods of coping.

Thankfully, we know the source of our hope. Through him, we will acquire the necessary strength and courage to cope not just with today but with all of our tomorrows as well.

> *Yet there is one ray of hope: his compassion never ends.* It is only the Lord's mercies that have kept us from complete destruction. Great is his faithfulness; his lovingkindness begins afresh each day. My soul claims the Lord as my inheritance; therefore I will hope in him. The Lord is wonderfully good to those who wait for him, to those who seek for him.
>
> **Lamentations 3:21-25**

Learning to cope is a long-term, ongoing project, but my last suggestion is one that will help right away. Purchase a pair of knitting needles (any size), an instruction booklet if you're a beginner, and a skein of beautifully colored yarn. Cast on a reasonable number of stitches and knit anything you can create out of a simple block of knitting—a scarf, a dish cloth, a baby blanket, a giant afghan you know you'll never finish. The therapy is not in the finished project or in a job well done but in the soothing rhythm of your hands as you work. There are probably many other activities that bring the same sense of peace and order to the brain, but the key is to keep it simple without a pattern or particular set of stitches. You should be able to listen, discuss, or even pray as you knit.

Certainly, there is no medical or otherwise preconceived outcome of this knitting activity. If there is any reason to its effectiveness, it's simply that it calms and quiets us so that we can hear God and wait patiently and hopefully.

Father God, forgive me for giving in to despair. Give me new hope and the ability to cope until my child and my situation are healed. Amen.

Confession

❧

My husband and I are often at odds
over our challenging child. It leaves us
feeling distant and unmarried.
The worst part is that we are so
very used to the feeling that it
doesn't even hurt anymore.

TWENTY-NINE

When You Start Blaming Your Spouse

DO YOU HARBOR THE SECRET of a "lost" marriage? A union devoid of sex, small talk, nights out, or even smiling? Have you reached the point that you're not even sure if you care? Yes? Not to worry, your secret is forever safe with me. Furthermore, I can absolutely assure you that many of us with a challenging child have felt or are currently feeling similar feelings of marital discord. It comes with the territory. I'm even going to take this idea one step further and suggest that perhaps your situation is not as serious as you think.

I present this bold concept to you because we are traveling a similar route. I know from experience that very often what we perceive as a problem can sometimes simply be a common characteristic of couples who produce challenging offspring. This characteristic is the tendency to establish a child-dominated marriage climate. It's not that I'm saying such a climate doesn't bring destruction to a husband-wife relationship, just that it is a fairly amenable state of affairs and not as devastating as it may now seem.

None of us purposely set out to establish such an arrangement. It's one of those things that just innocently happens when a baby is born. In the beginning, our helpless, adorable infant requires almost every ounce of our love and attention, and so we give it—freely and unselfishly. If at times it seems we'll never see the light at the end of the tunnel, we are encouraged as the child grows and voluntarily drops many of his demands and time-consuming needs. Slowly but surely, marriage and family life return to normal, and we all live happily ever after. Well, almost. A problem arises for some of us when the child is still demanding and dominating several years later.

Of course, one of the things we're dealing with in our unique situation is the personality of the challenging child. He is without question more demanding and dominating than the average youngster. He is without question more spirited and driven than his siblings. He is without question the star in his own little drama of daily life. After a few years of catering to this child's needs, a couple may be so accustomed to accommodating to his antics that they aren't even aware how inappropriate their lifestyle has become. An almost superficial marriage, for instance, may be an arrangement created through the years for survival. If it works, the idea of change is not always appealing. Why rock the boat?

Indeed, why should we bother to make changes that will call upon our last little bit of strength and require all of our remaining cool? Or put another way, why should we even care? Well, let me remind you why.

We should care because we love the child and because love is the touchstone in his ultimate healing. It's important that this particular child knows he is loved at home. When all the world is against him, he should always be able to count on the knowledge that home is where mom is waiting for him with outstretched arms. But it is also where this youngster should be observing the loving relationship between two other people—mom and dad. We should care because we love our husband, and because love is the cornerstone of the home and relationship we have built together.

Sadly, however, the needs of our child don't coincide well with the needs of our spouse. The greatest problems seem to be with parenting styles.

- *Our spouse thinks we're too lax.*
  We think he's too strict.

- *He thinks we lavish attention on the child.*
  We think he withholds.
- *He thinks we spend too much time on the child.*
  We think he spends too little.
- *He thinks we favor the child.*
  We think he openly dislikes the child.

The result in such conflict is that mother and child find themselves pitted against dad, instead of mother and dad countering the child. This is very wrong, not to mention quite dangerous to the marriage.

Children were never intended to be the center and focus of a family. The center of the family is the husband and wife relationship, with children complementing and completing the relationship.

> You wives, submit yourselves to your husbands, for that is what the Lord has planned for you. And you husbands must be loving and kind to your wives and not bitter against them, nor harsh. You children must always obey your fathers and mothers, for that pleases the Lord. Fathers, don't scold your children so much that they become discouraged and quit trying.
>
> **Colossians 3:18-21**

A modern woman may not like the tone of this Scripture, but there is a reason for God's order in the family. When a husband and wife focus primarily on their relationship, the entire family unit is sheltered by their love. Children are allowed to be children. Parents are expected to be authority figures. Each family member knows his place in the circle of love and is able to interact accordingly.

Of course, this picture of family life is not a popular view today. The media and academic circles like to talk about the diversity of family structure, and society is encouraged not only to tolerate various family structures but to applaud and uphold these groups of people who, by many standards, are living deviant lifestyles. Even though the world would have us think otherwise, we can see that the demise of the family has clearly given rise to many of today's problems. Teen crime, teen pregnancies, and teen drug usage are among the more visible scars of our country's deteriorating family structures. But just as serious are the problems society faces when teens leave high school without the basic knowledge needed to attend college or land an entry-level job.

What does this have to do with our challenging child versus the lack of a relationship with our spouse? Simply that children must spend time in the safety and structure of a close family unit in order to absorb values and acquire morals. When children live with only one parent, spend a part of each day under the care of someone other than a family member, or come home to an empty house after school, they not only must learn to function without adequate parental supervision, they never have the opportunity to learn by observation. It's frightening to think of the decisions children have to make on their own these days. Decisions as basic as whether or not to rob a convenience store or whether or not to have sex after school are ones that probably wouldn't have to be made if mom or dad were setting an example and present in the home.

Family life is a serious issue for all parents, but for those of us with a challenging child, the stakes are even higher. If we are truly seeking the best advantages for this child, our lives must be part of the solution, not part of the problem. In plain words, divorce and separation are never part of the solution, and they can in no way be of any help to our struggling child.

Jesus on divorce says:

> But it certainly isn't God's way. For from the very first he made man and woman to be joined together permanently in marriage; therefore a man is to leave his father and mother, and he and his wife are united so that they are no longer two, but one. And no man may separate what God has joined together.
>
> **Mark 10:7-9**

This is not a subject I like to write about—my own marriage is subject to such strong pressures. And yet, in many ways, I think only the mother of a challenging child can speak to another mother in this situation about the importance and difficulty of maintaining a good marriage while these children are at home.

Many times I find myself wondering if it's even possible to make significant changes at this stage of life. "I am who I am," I want to stubbornly declare. "If he doesn't like the way I am, or if the marriage can't work the way I am, too bad." But inside, I know there is both room and time for change—else why would I be on this journey? And so I continue to read and study and pray in search of answers. What I have learned so far is that a woman can be everything she has to be—no matter the situation—if she relies on divine guidance. And the decision to rely on this guidance may be the easiest step we take on the rest of our journey. Taking it removes the animosity, struggle, and anger we've been holding inside. Taking it enables us to love purely and completely. Taking it removes the impossible obstacles of hate, time, and fear. What do we have to do? Not much; just agree to put one foot out and take the step. God wants us to simply be. He will do the rest.

Here's how to get started:

1. Be a talker.

Parents of challenging children often find themselves angry at each other. Remember that we get angry because we care. We want our actions and beliefs to affirm our connection and commitment to each other. Disagreement can be just as affirming. Talk about your differences in parenting styles. Agree not to be competitive but to learn to act cooperatively (and then to share your frustration when it doesn't work.)

And now this word to all of you: You should be like one big happy family, full of sympathy toward each other, loving one another with tender hearts and humble minds.

1 Peter 3:8

2. Be generous.

Whether it's discipline, medication, or extracurricular activities, there are many times throughout the day when the way we interact with our challenging child causes a problem with our spouse. When it happens, apologize. (Even if it didn't seem like that big a deal to you.) Then tell your spouse exactly what you intend to do about it, and really work on doing it.

Be gentle and ready to forgive; never hold grudges. Remember, the Lord forgave you, so you must forgive others.

Colossians 3:13

3. Be respectful.

Because a challenging child routinely threatens our self-respect, a spouse's criticism can seem like further attack. We are hurt, and the most logical action that comes to mind is striking back. We want to hurt our partner for making us hurt. But it's respect that will keep us centered and moving forward on our journey. Look for ways to build a sense of personal worth and self-respect. Here are a few ideas to build on:

- *You have made it to this point.*
- *You are a cherished child of God.*
- *You have been given a job (your challenging child) requiring above average skills and capabilities.*

Respect the fact that both you and your husband are struggling. This is not an easy time for either of you. When you are so angry that hurting back feels like the only just and honest reaction, try not to react but to say what you feel without emotions getting in the way. Mutual respect at times of adversity doesn't magically happen; it is built on love over a period of time.

4. Be satisfied.

Isn't there enough "bad" in the world without looking for it? Vow today to stop looking for imperfections in your mate. Instead, look for the good, for the parts of that person that you wanted and needed in a husband way back when. They're still there.

Sometimes we blame our spouse for everything that's wrong. We are empty and lonely and angry because our life has been inconvenienced by a challenging child, and we look beyond the child toward our spouse. He could make it better, we reason, with a new house, a more attentive attitude, a more loving disposition. The truth is, none of these things will replace the healing of our child. So put such longings aside. Seeing things as they really are may make us uncomfortable, but it also empowers us to find the help we need while being grateful for what we have.

Let him have all your worries and cares, for he is always thinking about you and watching everything that concerns you.

1 Peter 5:7

5. Be a peacemaker.

During this time of fragile family life, see to it that ordinary couples' squabbles are not in your repertoire. Which television shows to watch, how to spend money, what to do on weekends, and whether to go out or stay home should not be high concerns when a challenging child is tearing you apart. Give up the little power struggles to give your mind the room to concentrate on building a strong relationship with your spouse.

None of the problems that arise between a husband and wife while struggling with a challenging child are because we don't love each other but because we're not always sure what to do with what we know about that love. We look at our challenging child and see a person no one else finds quite acceptable. To us, there may seem no alternative but to continue the unhealthy, symbiotic, mother-child relationship we have going.

However, I encourage you to put such feelings aside. None of the temporary peace you may gain at the moment will benefit you or your child in the future. He will need to master the careful balance of loving and living to get himself successfully through the adventures of life. And it is no coincidence that such balance is best learned under the umbrella of a harmonious husband and wife team. God created the family because it works. Family values within the framework of marriage can influence and make the difference in young lives. Within the nurturing, protective realm of a happy marriage, children learn to adjust to life—the good and the bad, the pain and the joy. This is the atmosphere you want to place your challenging child in and the environment that will bring you greatest happiness as well.

While God does endorse the family as the preferred environment in which to raise a family, he never says the burden is all on us. For the difficult times, he has given us the Comforter.

If you are the mother of a challenging child, you cannot afford to overlook this tremendous resource. When your world is falling apart and your private life holds secrets of bitterness and hate, call upon the Holy Spirit. Through him, you can learn to love anyway. He can open your eyes to all that is good and true about your spouse. He can heal your attitude and heart until you see your marriage from a spiritually renewed perspective.

Even if your marriage problems seem beyond hope, defeat need not be the outcome. Where there is God, there is hope. I particularly want you to know that no matter where you are and what you are doing, God is with you. Furthermore, he has a plan just for you that no one else can fulfill. Perhaps the exact plan will never be revealed to you as such, but be assured that God will be guiding you toward it, step by step, day by day. Look for his guidance through Scripture study. Ask for his guidance through prayer.

Just as your child is a product of God's handiwork, your marriage is an act of his perfect creation. Surely, such a creation deserves to be cherished, nurtured, and uplifted through prayer. Surely such a creation deserves to be honored by every expression of your daily life. This is the price of love, and it is never too much.

Two can accomplish more than twice as much as one, for the results can be much better. If one falls, the other pulls him up; but if a man falls when he is alone, he's in trouble.

Ecclesiastes 4:9-10

Her children stand and bless her; so does her husband. He praises her with these words: "There are many fine women in the world, but you are the best of them all!"

Proverbs 31:28-29

A Practical Idea Strengthening a marriage can be a formidable challenge to a couple without the luxury of private time. If the ideas presented in this chapter seem idealistic to you, concentrate on first finding "couple time" once a month. This does not have to be a night on the town with dinner and the movies. My husband and I joined a parent support group that meets once a month and often use this meeting night as our date night. (For some reason, it's easier to find a baby-sitter, even for a hard-to-manage child, when people know you're doing something therapeutic or educational.) In addition to enjoying the atmosphere of these adult-only meetings, we always add the element of courtship to the evening by stopping on the way home for coffee or fat-free yogurt. It's amazing how much better things look after this break from routine.

Dear God, bless my marriage and our home. Protect our love from harmful influences. Amen.

Confession

❦

I grieve for a certain type of
relationship I don't have
with my child.

THIRTY

Dream Scenes

MAKING COOKIES, GOING TO THE THEATER, buying a toy at the toy store—they are all dream scenes for the mother of a challenging child because certainly there is little chance of her ever successfully completing such an activity with her youngster. Somewhere in the back of her mind is the cherished childhood memory of a happy time shared with a special person—a memory still so warm and inviting that she would like to make it a reality again with her child. Or perhaps there is no happy memory; just the knowledge of what could have been versus what really was. Now she wants to make it right by giving to her child what wasn't given to her. Alas, the challenging child isn't sentimental when it comes to behavior, and he's not buying any of mom's ideas for a good time.

Baking cookies becomes a full-scale disaster complete with flour and icing spread from wall to wall. This child doesn't listen to instructions, doesn't want to be like mom, and loses interest as soon as the mess gets overwhelming. Going to the theater proves a mistake that mom finds embarrassing and uncomfortable when he talks out loud and makes continuous trips to the bathroom. Perhaps he will threaten to or actually throw a tantrum to get his way about something improper like sitting on the arm of his seat. And as for going to a toy store, only a mother in denial would be so foolish as to attempt such a feat with her challenging child. Of course we all do, now and then, because it is part of our dream. But what a mother may have imagined as a shared delight soon becomes a nightmare when this child loudly demands one expensive thing after another, calling mom names, kicking over displays, grabbing at everything.

Our grief after such episodes is profound. Like a barren woman, we feel cheated and sad. The child we dreamed of is not here.

No. But the child of God's dreams is, and if we are hurting right now, it is only because our human expectations have let us down. We wanted a child who fit our description of the perfect son or daughter who would do the things we imagined in our way. But if we think we know what would make the perfect child, shouldn't God know even better?

"And if even sinful persons like yourselves give children what they need, don't you realize that your heavenly Father will do at least as much, and give the Holy Spirit to those who ask for him?"

Luke 11:13

There is nothing wrong with having high expectations for our child or anticipating a certain event we will share with him. We just need to be careful that our expectations and anticipations are for the glory of God, not ourselves. For instance, instead of visualizing a cozy scene in which you are enjoying being with your child, picture a scene in which you are loving the child. Experts tell us that children learn best by modeling. So model love. Model patience. Model joy. Decide ahead of time how much disruption you can gracefully handle, and close the activity before the mess or the rowdy behavior gets the best of your disposition. Be prepared for possible mishaps and plan accordingly. Another way to conduct successful activities with challenging children is to allow them to participate in only a portion of the event. Decorating the cookies, not mixing and baking them. Leaving a play at intermission. Going to only one section of the toy store.

Perhaps God doesn't intend for us to do any of the standard activities with this child. But that doesn't mean your dreams have been shattered, only that you haven't fully realized them. Oh, yes, I know about the baby who would never let you rock him but arched his back and stiffened in your arms. I know about the good times that became full of anger and hurt. I, too, have looked at sweet little children sitting beside their moms at church and questioned the fairness of life as my own child noisily disturbed everyone around us.

Sometimes it helps to remember that there are special moments with a challenging child that other moms will never have. Such moments are as different and varied as the children themselves—an especially keen insight, a deep sensitivity at a moment of crisis, an unusual ability or skill. Cherish these moments by imprinting them in your memory. At such times you are close to God's dream for you, and life is beginning to make sense.

> I pray that your hearts will be flooded with light so that you can see something of the future he has called you to share.
>
> **Ephesians 1:18a**

A Practical Idea Remember that as your child is healed, he is in the process of becoming. You can help determine the type of person he will become by always thinking of him in the highest possible light. Here are important pointers to keep in mind.

- *Your child will absorb your perceptions of him.* Start carrying a mental picture of an adorable, lovable version of him in your mind.

- *Your child will become an expression of his activities.* Turn him into a helping person by letting him participate in as many "helping" activities as possible. Even a child with a very short attention span can sign his name to Christmas cards for nursing home residents, help sort old clothing for charity, or help deliver Cokes to the employees at dad's office. Think of all the simple ways your child can contribute to the lives of others and organize one helping activity a month.

- *Your child will get what he expects from life.* Teach him to expect the best. No matter how many bad experiences the two of you have had, always voice the belief that "something good is going to happen this time."

Dear Father, give me the courage and love to raise this special child and to realize I am fulfilling your dream for me. Amen.

Confession

❦

I have done everything I know to do.
I feel as if I can do nothing more
for my child.

THIRTY-ONE

"Why Did I Wait So Long?"

SOMETIMES AFTER TRYING EVERYTHING WE KNOW TO DO with a challenging child, we seem to be met with defeat. It's as if there is nothing further we can do to help our child. You are at this point on your journey of life if you are thinking about giving up, letting the child go his way behaviorally, giving full reign to unsympathetic authority figures, or simply resigning yourself to the child's failure.

However, I am happy to tell you there is absolutely no need for despair at this point. You are not really at the end of the road. This rock bottom place in your life is more like another beginning—a place for regrouping, rethinking your plan, and adopting new strategy. Now you know that you are, in fact, not going to reach this child through conventional words and actions. Now you are finally ready to earnestly pursue prayer.

There are many ways to help meet the emotional needs of a troubled child, but I believe that if a true transformation is part of God's plan for the child, it is very likely to come about as a result of his parents' prayers. Why do I believe this? Because I have a strong personal history of answered prayer.

One of the earliest of these memories is of my childhood in Nigeria where my parents were missionaries. I happened to want a Barbie doll for my tenth birthday, and so I asked God for one. This was quite a daring request, given the fact that there were no dolls for sale, period, in Nigeria at that time.

Also, a high import duty dictated that we only receive toys in the mail at Christmas.

For weeks I privately prayed for my Barbie, but by the night before my birthday I had become so desperate that I told God I would accept any doll. The next morning there was no Barbie doll, but to my great delight, my older sister had painstakingly crafted a doll from paper mâché. I knew without a doubt that God had made my sister receptive to my need, and even though I was only a child, I remember being very aware of having dabbled with a mighty power.

Years later, when my husband and I were both in school, we once found ourselves in fairly severe financial straits. One day we were facing particularly bad problems. An eviction notice had been put on the door of our inexpensive student house because the lot it was on was to become a parking lot. Our checking account held fifty dollars to find new housing and buy the month's groceries. I decided to spend it on the groceries. As I got into the car, my eyes filled with tears.

"Let's pray," my oldest daughter, who was then four years old said.

I remember turning to her and replying, "We can't pray for this—this is really serious!"

But, of course, we did. And miraculously, even for those days, our groceries lasted until my husband and I found a summer job as camp directors that paid a salary plus provided room and board.

Another remarkable answer to prayer occurred a few years ago when my husband and I were undergoing the stress of a failed business partnership. Again, we found ourselves in a financial bind with only limited time to make serious decisions. When my parents prayed for a solution, I only halfheartedly joined in. But when a headhunter called my husband—cold—for a job that was perfectly suited to his training, I knew the real source of our care once more.

There have been physical healings within our family as well.

When my first child was born with a head that bordered on hydrocephalic proportions, my husband and I prayed a year for its correction. Today she is a perfectly beautiful and highly intelligent young woman. In addition to this miracle, my husband and I have experienced the healing of one parent from cancer and rejoiced when another survived the rigors of a heart attack.

These experiences, as well as many others just like them, have caused me to put great faith in prayer. Even though not every prayer has been answered to my liking, and some appear not to have been answered at all, the overall benefits of praying have been far greater than the disappointment I may have felt at those times when God clearly said no.

Maybe you aren't so sure. It's been a long time since you've prayed. Perhaps you have never prayed. Maybe you did and nothing happened. At this moment, you are thinking you don't know why you should begin praying now, and that if you did, you wouldn't know where to begin.

Personally, I think it helps to begin the process by knowing that prayer is going to help you in these ways:

- **Prayer provides peace of mind.**

- **Prayer is communication with God.** It's you talking to God and God talking to you. You need someone to talk to.

- **Prayer provides answers to your problems.** Solutions that come to us as a result of prayer are divinely inspired and are often ideas or thoughts we wouldn't have come up with on our own. You do have problems that haven't yet been solved.

  This plan of mine is not what you would work out, neither are my thoughts the same as yours! For just as the heavens are higher than the earth, so are my ways higher than yours, and my thoughts than yours.   **Isaiah 55:8-9**

- **Prayer helps us surrender to God.** Until we have given up our way for God's way, we are not going to find the right direction for our journey with this child. You have a struggle you need to give up on.

There are not many people who would willingly pass up these wonderful benefits of prayer, but sometimes even those of us who know about them forego our good out of ignorance. We are afraid we don't know how to pray. Prayer, to us, is a strange, mystical activity that only the very saintly can do properly. We, in our own judgment, are not pious enough, religious enough, nor good enough to converse with God.

Of course we have it all wrong. In practice, prayer is an ordinary, everyday thing—a simple exercise of the heart and mind that just happens to be holy and powerful as well. Thankfully, there are no religious requirements for prayer. God takes us anywhere and in any condition. We can cry and complain or praise and give thanks—God always listens and always cares. The psalmist, David, shows us again and again that prayer is conversation of a meaningful, realistic nature.

> Come, Lord, and show me your mercy, for I am helpless, overwhelmed, in deep distress; my problems go from bad to worse. Oh, save me from them all! See my sorrows; feel my pain; forgive my sins. **Psalm 25:16-18**

> I plead with you to help me, Lord, for you are my Rock of safety. If you refuse to answer me, I might as well give up and die. **Psalm 28:1**

> It is good to say "Thank you" to the Lord, to sing praises to the God who is above all gods. **Psalm 92:1**

David helps us see that our human nature is not too "common" for the ear of God. Many of his prayers were taught to us as children in Sunday school, and we are amazed when a particular incident brings the Scripture back to us word for word. Psalm 23 is a favorite. This paraphrased excerpt from the *Living Bible* may bring the passage to life for you once again:

Because the Lord is my Shepherd, I have everything I need! He lets me rest in the meadow grass and leads me beside the quiet streams. He restores my failing health. He helps me do what honors him the most. Even when walking through the dark valley of death I will not be afraid, for you are close beside me, guarding, guiding all the way. You provide delicious food for me in the presence of my enemies. You have welcomed me as your guest; blessings overflow! Your goodness and unfailing kindness shall be with me all of my life, and I will live with you forever in your home.

Psalm 23

Later, Jesus taught the disciples another special prayer that is still used by Christians today. Although the following paraphrased version may be different, you will undoubtedly recognize the words:

And this is the prayer he taught them: "Father, may your name be honored for its holiness; send your Kingdom soon. Give us our food day by day. And forgive our sins—for we have forgiven those who sinned against us. And don't allow us to be tempted." **Luke 11:2-4**

Even after recognizing and reclaiming these old Scripture friends, you may still feel self-conscious about praying from your heart. If this is true, start by giving yourself a few moments of quiet time. Quiet your mind and allow the Holy Spirit to teach you from within. You may feel prompted to sing a song of praise, perhaps one from childhood. You may want to repeat a Scripture or a simple thought such as, "God is with me now." The main thing is to relax and pray in your own way, knowing that God is listening no matter the method or the words used. Of course, just as you will be asking others to pray for your child, always remember to include in your quiet time a prayer for other challenging children.

When we pray, we are working with God, for our prayers

are an important part of "God care." God care is care that is full of love and encouragement. It is gentle and soothing, peaceful and calming. Most important, it is powerful. Our prayers make it so.

A Practical Idea Develop your prayer life by starting a prayer ministry. Praying for others will give you a sense of purpose and is something concrete you can do for others regardless of your situation. I share such a ministry with my challenging child. Wherever we go, she collects business cards (a great activity for busy, restless hands), and we pray for these strangers by name each morning, asking God to help them in whatever way they need help. It's a lot of fun to imagine the good these people are receiving as we visualize God's blessings pouring down on them.

Dear Father, teach me to pray with depth. I want to give the best in "God care." Teach me to come to you first, and to teach my child to come to you as well. Amen.

Confession

❧

I am feeling very angry at people for past
injustices committed toward my child.
I want to hurt someone back.

THIRTY-TWO

❦

When Revenge Starts to Look Good

LOOKING BACK CAN BE PAINFUL for the mothers of challenging children. Our hearts often carry pockets of hidden bitterness as a result of past hurts: teachers who were openly cruel to our child, doctors who were not forthcoming with a correct diagnosis, children who excluded and mocked our child, and strangers who refused to accommodate his special needs. The list could go on and on. Certainly our anger does.

Understand that this is a different type of anger than you might have felt toward your child at times. Though you might not always have responded the way you wanted to at those times, you did at least respond. On the contrary, your anger at the "system" has no place to go. Perhaps you've recently discovered an injustice committed on your child years ago. You are not even certain enough of the facts to pursue legal action. Maybe it is a situation out of your control. You were in a public place, and a stranger did something to hurt your child before you realized it was happening. Or maybe it involves the issue of age. The people who wronged your child were children so you didn't say anything because you felt uncomfortable in their domain.

Though all anger should be released, past injustices can come back to torment us again and again. The question of whether to reopen the issue or lay the matter to rest rises each time we are reminded of our child's rights by the media, teachers, or various professionals. When do we know when a particular action or inaction is the right thing to do?

I believe that when the outcome of our action will in some way serve others and benefit the lives of challenging children and their families, we can be fairly sure we are following God's path. (This would be a reasonable guideline by which to judge the worthiness of legal action.) At other times, we know God's will is simply for us to do nothing.

Sometimes God clearly wants us to use this anger to further a good cause. Think about it. If you're battling unresolved anger, why not use the energy behind it to push for community rights or to organize help that could aid other people rearing challenging children. God equips us for everything we need to fulfill our job here on earth. Maybe some of us need the energy of anger to get something started.

The interesting thing is that when we do become involved in championing a cause, we find we're no longer dwelling on the source of our anger but are now focusing on the challenge of a project. The ultimate goal of releasing those bad feelings has finally come about.

Of course, you don't have to have a vindicated past in order to be happy. You can be happy because you know God will eventually right every wrong, and your good will one day be established. But you must also remember that just as God is working on your behalf, he is also working for the fellow who caused your misery. God is for both of you, and the moment this truth becomes clear to you, the struggle to "fix things" and the problem of dealing with your anger will be over. Congratulations. You have given your burden to God. From this point on, you will not slip or fall.

Give your burdens to the Lord. He will carry them. He will not permit the godly to slip or fall.   **Psalm 55:22**

A Practical Idea You don't have to sue or publicly protest in order to use your hurtful experiences for the benefit of others. Why not volunteer as a consultant for parents undergoing similar problems? Give your name and phone number to your child's physician who can then pass it on to parents in need. You might also place it on a bulletin board in an environment you trust, such as your church. I am not suggesting you offer counseling services; these are better left in the hands of professionals. Your offer should be for the guidance and direction of parents who don't know what to do next when choosing a school, looking for friends, or confronting some type of discrimination. Your help could even be as simple as forming a private lending library in which you share your books and articles with other searching parents. Remember how eagerly you read and how hard you hunted for more to read when your child was first diagnosed?

God is working to turn everything that happens to you into a blessing. Look for him in everything.

Dear God, I forgive those who have hurt me and my child. I ask you now to help me use the formerly pent up energy for the good of all children who meet daily challenges. Amen.

Confession

❧

I feel sorry for myself,
and my sorrow is like
falling into a great pit
I can't get out of.

THIRTY-THREE

❦

Mothers Are a Sorry Lot

MOST TIMES, THE MEMORY OF A SIMPLE SMILE or a warm embrace are all it takes to convince me that motherhood has been a wise and wonderful choice. These are the crowning moments of motherhood that even the mother of a challenging child can claim.

There are other moments of mothering that are not so happy. Perhaps for you there was a time when the school called to say your child was being sent home for bad behavior. Maybe there was a time your child couldn't interact properly with his birthday party guests, and everyone left in a huff. Or maybe there was a time your child refused to obey and even said he hated you. These are the experiences we remember with pain and a sense of loss. These are the times we need comfort and an extra measure of love.

It's possible you are going through such a time right now; if so, I am truly sorry and sympathetic because I've had such days myself.

Only recently I left my daughter at a day camp, thinking it would give me the freedom and opportunity to spend some quality time with one of my sisters. And it did. But when I returned I was met with this note:

To the guardian of Alexandra:
Alexandra missed out on bowling today due to her consistent attitude problem. She frequently challenges our authority and shows no willingness to change her actions.

She stirs up the other children to rebel against camp rules and is consistently pushing us to see where we will draw the line.

Perhaps only the mother of another challenging child could know how devastated I felt at that moment. Suddenly I was undergoing all the pain and humiliation I had ever suffered because of my child's behavior. The imaginary parade of teachers, mothers, and other people who had once made similar remarks to me marched across my mind with victory while a taunting little voice inside of me made threatening remarks: "You're never going to be able to depend on her to behave. It's never going to get better. You're only kidding yourself when you say she's improved."

I went to my room and lay down. I was a tired, broken woman, but not nearly as discouraged as I once would have been. For after going through this type of thing for several years now, I knew that Christ's love would give me all the comfort and peace necessary to restore my heart and soul to wholeness. And sure enough, in a little while I was able to get up and meet my daughter's question, "Are you mad at me?" with a smile.

Christ will give this measure of comfort to you as well if you ask for it. Whatever may be happening in life his love can become your refuge. His presence in your life can fill your heart with comfort and with the knowledge that you are not alone, and that you can make it through whatever crisis you may be facing right now.

Difficult times are never something we look forward to. Yet we know that our worst times are often marked by an increased spiritual awareness. It has helped me to embrace such periods of pain as an invitation to a special retreat with God—a retreat in which every minute is guaranteed to provide me with new strength and fresh insights. But I have not found it easy, and so I offer these little suggestions for easing pain and bringing comfort:

Little things that add comfort:

1. **Begin the day with uplifting music**—classical, spiritual, or Broadway hits. Choose something that makes you feel alive and happy, and fill your home with these sounds rather than the television or radio.

2. **Surround yourself with things you love that make you feel close to God.** Keep your Bible, a favorite inspirational book, and a notepad nearby so that you can turn to these resources in free moments. Wear a piece of jewelry that has special significance to your spiritual journey. If you don't own such a piece, choose this moment of discovering God's love as your milestone and purchase some type of religious jewelry to mark it.

3. **Make contact with a friend you can count on.**

4. **Drink plenty of fluids.** Eat fresh foods, close to their natural state. Take a nap or go to bed early.

5. **Wear your favorite comfortable clothing** that makes you look and feel especially attractive.

6. **Do something creative** such as making a simple quilt for snuggling into on cold days.

It's not always easy to be patient as we wait for Christ to comfort us. But we know he will, because he said so.

I will comfort you there as a little one is comforted by its mother.

Isaiah 66:13

Those of us who have been fortunate to have a caring, nurturing mother know that a mother offers a certain kind of comfort. She does not use the moment of distress for lectures and reprimands but genuinely empathizes with her child's sorrow. She makes some type of physical contact—perhaps a patting of the back or a stroking of the head. She offers gentle reassurances with such words as, "There, there," or, "Now, now." She is the pillar of strength for her child to lean on, the place of refuge where everything is all right. This is the kind of comfort Jesus offers us. When we are down, and our cup seems a little less than full, Jesus reminds us that it is not exactly empty, and that soon, very soon, it will become full and overflowing with the joy of life.

A Practical Idea If you don't keep a journal, start one today. In the front of your book, make a list of activities that will brighten your day. The next time you are feeling gloomy and sad, choose one of these activities to lift your mood. Here are a few ideas to get you started:

- *Paint an old piece of furniture* with the color that cheers you most.

- *Open the curtains, raise the shades, or turn on the lamps*—everything looks better in the light.

- *Re-read your favorite childhood chapter book.*

- *Draw beautiful flowers* on the inside cover page of your Bible.

Little things, to be sure, but sometimes it's actions such as these that help us to relax and accept the comforting presence of God's love.

Yes, your cup of joy will overflow!

John 15:11b

Dear God, let me feel your joy. Help me share it with others. I love you. Amen.

Confession

❦

I am confused about healing.
Is there a difference between being cured
and being healed?
I really want my child to be well—
not just okay in the sight
of the Lord.
But when do I give up?

THIRTY-FOUR
~~~

Be Healed!

SOMETIMES THE REQUEST FOR OUR CHILD'S HEALING seems to open up a can of worms we aren't quite sure how to handle. People's questions, accusations, and confrontations about the healing process can leave our minds so befuddled that we begin to feel as if our personal integrity is dependent upon our child's success. To make matters worse, somewhere deep within the hidden recesses of our innermost thoughts lies a fear about healing that is so dreadful, so horrifying, so very likely— that we dare not let it see the light of day. This is the fear that our child may not be healed after all.

"What happens then?" we ask ourselves when this fear comes to the forefront of our thoughts. Do we have to acknowledge that we have failed in our request? In our faith? In our inability to make a healing out of hopelessness? How do we explain to our friends the apparent inaction of a deity whom we have always referred to as "a loving God?" How do we go on believing when it means we must also go on suffering? Such are the everyday thoughts of a mother on the quest for her challenging child's highest good.

All believers would probably agree that when one has requested healing, depending on God's will being done, there is always a healing in some form. But let's face it. If we have envisioned a physical healing, few of us are really accepting of the situation when after months or years of praying and believing, we still don't have the normally functioning child we asked for.

If this is where you are today, it may be too soon to talk about acceptance and finding the joy in your sorrow. In fact, perhaps the apparent lack of healing you perceive is nothing more than an issue of time and a matter of impatience. Remember, every healing is a miracle, whether it happens instantaneously in a flash of glory or over a long, slow period of time. And all healing comes from God whether it occurs mysteriously by prayer alone or after a well-documented series of treatments administered by health professionals. When we remove preconceived ideas about the physical characteristics of healing, we see that there is no time limit or particular means by which it comes about.

It's also true that accepting the child as he is now and receiving God's gift of abundant living in the midst of difficulty is a healing that enables us to go forward with life. For many of us, this type of healing is so satisfying that we want nothing more. But if you are a mother who wants to keep on seeking a physical healing, even when the evidence is not encouraging, you, too, are within your biblical "rights."

Unless your child has died, your journey is not over. As long as you are both alive and as long as you seek your child's healing, you must keep praying.

Though some people believe we should ask only once, because to do otherwise shows a lack of faith, the Bible says no such thing. In Luke 18:1-8, Jesus tells the parable of the persistent widow who keeps going back to the judge to request justice against her adversary. For a long time the judge refused. Finally, he gave her the justice she sought because her persistence was so annoying. Jesus told this story to his disciples to teach them they should not stop praying just because the answer appears to be no.

When we begin asking for a physical healing we can't tell what God's will is going to be. God is the one who makes the decision. So to keep praying for the healing without results does not violate God's will. At this point, we truly don't know what his will is.

Perhaps the answer *is* no. For whatever reason, God wants our child to stay just the way he is. But we can only know this by seeing our child's life from beginning to end.

Some of us will feel a sense of obligation to keep seeking a physical healing throughout our child's life. Fortunately, time is on our side because God promises to complete the good work he began in our children at birth. This is no guarantee that he sees a physical healing as a necessary part of completion, but it certainly leaves us every reason to hope.

Occasionally, we are confronted with a challenge that defies the idea of a physical healing, such as in the case of a mentally retarded child. What can we ask for when physical evidence overpowers any rational request for a physical healing? The answer is still a physical healing.

We can ask for a physical healing with the understanding that each new activity and ability gained by this child is a type of restoration and renewal. While medical texts might say otherwise, we really can't put limitations on any child because we don't know the full extent of his capabilities until his life is completed. Indeed, some of these special children acquire skills far surpassing the predictions of medical and educational experts.

In the meantime, a praying parent of such a child will undoubtedly receive his own personal healing. This is a healing from the pain and anger that first accompanied the child's diagnosis. For with or without a physical change, healing takes place whenever we accept God's divine plan for our lives. While we look toward God for outward changes in our children, we see that nothing ever changes the existence of God or takes away the harmony and peace he brings with an inner healing.

And so it is with prayer—keep on asking and you will keep on getting.

Luke 11:9a

A Practical Idea The best answers to our questions about healing always come from the Bible. If you know what the Bible says about healing but are still feeling confused, ask a trusted spiritual leader, such as your pastor, for clarification.

Dear God, heal my child in the way you know is best for her. And help me to be at peace with your will. Amen.

Confession:

I have to admit that it's easier to write about living with the challenging child than to live the life.

THIRTY-FIVE

~~~❦~~~

The Rest of the Way

PART OF ME WOULD LIKE TO STAY within the pages of this book forever, but my daughter pokes her head around the door, telling me that "something bad" has happened to her in my absence. I know from experience this could be anything from furniture polish splashed on the walls and doors of her room to super glue in her hair. So I am forced to return to the rigors of being a real-life mom. I suspect you are at that point, too. In fact, coming to the end of this book is like reaching a fork in the road on our shared journey.

Now each of us must go our own way. Instead of reading about the love and care of our challenging child, we will soon be facing the complexities of putting this love into action. However, we willingly allow this adventure to come to us because it is our calling. The experience itself is not new (some of us have been managing a challenging child for a long time), but the manner in which we accept it is fresh and exciting. For on this day, those of us who walk with God move forth with the knowledge that his love and power will see us through to the end.

By his grace we find ourselves able to be all that we need to be for our child. More loving. More patient. More flexible. More creative. More forgiving. Every moment of heartbreak and struggle can now be replaced with joy and strength. God has taken a difficult situation and made it into something good.

A Prayer For the Challenging Child

Dear God,

This is a prayer for children who can never find their shoes.
Who throw tantrums in the grocery store and sulk in the car.
Who scream at their parents and hit their friends.

This is a prayer for children who rattle papers in church.
Who stick gum to their eyelashes and draw pictures on their skin.
Who kick bashful cats and eat from the dog's bowl.

This is a prayer for children who don't like to be hugged.
Who wad up their math homework and throw it away.
Who don't match their clothes well and have tangles in their hair.

This is a prayer for children who yell into the telephone.
Who say funny things and cause us to laugh.
Who fall asleep at midnight and wake up at dawn.

This is a prayer for children who won't color in the lines.
Who read Shakespeare and Dickens but can't learn their math.
Who can learn their math, but can't read their text.

This is a prayer for children who are afraid of the dark but believingly
    pray for the presence of your angels.
This is a prayer for children who love you.

Heal them, God. Bless them.
Protect them. Forgive them.
But most of all, just love them, Father.
Because this is a prayer for children whom the world has never
    greeted with enthusiasm nor cherished as a treasure.
Though surely, as your creations, they do deserve both.

So this is a prayer to say thank you, dear God,
For putting these children here on our earth.
May we bring honor and glory to your name as we guide
    them along this part of their journey.

Amen.

Making a Treasure Map

A TREASURE MAP IS A SUCCESS CHART on which one's goals are depicted in a collage format. The "map" often has words describing the goal in terms of having already been achieved. If, for instance, your goal is to help your child learn to manage her impulsiveness, you might state it like this: "Suzy is good-natured and pleasant. She thinks before she acts." The pictures surrounding your statement might show children playing happily and working cheerfully together.

If you want to work on really having a good time with your child, you might select pictures of parents playing and laughing with their children to go with a statement like this: "God shows me how to have fun with Bobby. We are courteous and kind to each other while playing." My own treasure map features the picture of a little girl wearing a wig and sunglasses. Beneath it is the caption: "Alexandra is God's perfect, beautiful child. She retains her individuality while becoming one with the world." For this is truly how I see her in the future—a spunky, creative person who can function well in the world.

People have different ideas as to what a treasure map is and how it should be used. Let me make it perfectly clear that I do not believe there is any magic in the process. Treasure mapping is simply a visual tool to remind us of the treasures God still has in store for us. Use it during times of meditation or place it where it will catch your eye on a daily basis. As you look at it, read your goal or goals out loud. The Bible tells us that what we say can become truth.

> Then Jesus told them, "Truly, if you have faith, and don't doubt, you can do things like this and much more. You can even say to this Mount of Olives, 'Move over into the ocean'; and it will." **Matthew 21:21**

APPENDIX B

Making a Name-Your-Day Book

A NAME-YOUR-DAY BOOK is an old Sunday school activity that is linked with the biblical account of Creation. Based on the idea that as Adam named things in the garden of Eden they became his, this little book will help you gain control over the chaos in your life by naming the condition you desire.

Choose one of the beautifully decorated blank books now on the market. At the top of each page write the date and the name you have given it. Miracle day, achievement day, success day, and high energy day are just some of the words you might use to describe your desired day. End your day by writing a blurb about your expectations and perhaps an account of how the day actually went.

Even a very young child can participate in this activity, though you may want to take dictation from a child who struggles with writing. The lesson in this exercise is that perfect days and golden opportunities are always out there, just waiting to be named. Eventually your child will see life as you do, that it isn't just a matter of staking a claim; we also have to reach out and follow that claim to the possibilities it suggests.

APPENDIX C

꧂

Special Helps:
Comfort from Scripture

God hears our prayers:

> And we are sure of this, that he will listen to us whenever we ask him for anything in line with his will. And if we really know he is listening when we talk to him and make our requests, then we can be sure that he will answer us.
>
> **1 John 5:14-15**

God is there to help:

> The Lord lifts the fallen and those bent beneath their loads.
>
> **Psalm 145:14**

It pays to keep a positive frame of mind:

> Fix your thoughts on what is true and good and right. Think about things that are pure and lovely, and dwell on the fine, good things in others. Think about all you can praise God for and be glad about. Keep putting into practice all you learned from me and saw me doing, and the God of peace will be with you.   **Philippians 4:8b-9**

The best is yet to come:

> Yet what we suffer now is nothing compared to the glory he will give us later.   **Romans 8:18**

God expects us to give him our best:

> Are you called to help others? Do it with all the strength and energy that God supplies, so that God will be glorified through Jesus Christ—to him be glory and power forever and ever. Amen.   **1 Peter 4:1b**